Born to Flow

Born to Flow® (BTF) is an invitation to rediscover flow, not as a fixed theory, but as a lived, evolving experience. Blending personal insight, practical wisdom, and inspiration from thinkers as diverse as Alan Watts, Bruce Lee, Rick Rubin, George Kelly, and Joseph Campbell, BTF explores flow as something you curate, not control.

Drawing on the river metaphor and Mihaly Csikszentmihalyi's work, BTF expands the conversation to include friction, creativity, and the journey of self-expression. It invites readers to release assumptions, embrace experimentation, and grow – not through perfection, but presence.

Like water shaping rock, flow emerges through sustained engagement. Insight, tools, and reflective practices offer a fresh hypothesis, guiding leaders, coaches, and creatives towards meaningful, grounded action. Applications include flow-aligned habits, navigating resistance, and creating environments for deep work. BTF is a dynamic framework to reclaim rhythm, honour creativity, and unlock inner potential.

Cliff Kimber holds an MSc in Coaching and Development from the University of Portsmouth and is a Fellow of the Institute of Leadership and the Royal Society of Arts. He coaches senior leaders and high-net-worth individuals (HNWIs) and is committed to individuals meeting their better selves.

'Cliff Kimber takes us all one step closer to owning and developing our flow. Discovering the beauty in the journey to embody the flow within. If the goal was the democratisation of flow, *Born to Flow* moves us all closer'.

Claire Davey, *Executive coach, former*
Head of Coaching at Deloitte UK

'In *Born to Flow*, Cliff masterfully blends psychology, philosophy, and personal experience. It returns us to something beautiful and primal: recognizing Flow is not a rare state, but the way life moves through us when we trust, align, and let go'.

Adam Karaoguz,
Former Navy SEAL

'Cliff Kimber's insights on flow have the power to change the way we experience life and help us transform the world we live in. His understandings offer us all access to deeper dimensions of who we are, our performance, our growth, evolution and engagement. So, if your potential is precious to you and living fully important then *Born to Flow* needs to be in your reading list'.

Jonny Wilkinson, *Founder at One Living,*
England Rugby International, RWC winner

'This is a book readers can return to again and again'.

Steve Borthwick,
England Head Coach, RFU

'*Born to Flow* is transformational. Cliff doesn't just explore flow, he redefines it. With warmth and insight, he challenges our hidden assumptions and reconnects us not just with our potential at work, but also ourselves, those who matter, and our lives. This isn't just for high achievers, it's for anyone seeking a more fully lived life'.

David Ross, *Fragile World Strategist,*
award winning author of Confronting the Storm

'I think that flow is always present, as long as you're alive! Cliff Kimber, a brilliant coach, trusted advisor and iconoclast, introduced this idea to me'.

Myles Downey, *Author of* Effective Coaching,
Lessons from the Coach's Coach

Born to Flow

A Way of Being

Cliff Kimber

Routledge
Taylor & Francis Group

LONDON AND NEW YORK

Designed cover image: Flow, 2014, oil on canvas, 106 x 106 cm, 42 x 42 in. Copyright Iain Faulkner, Courtesy of Pontone Gallery.

First published 2026
by Routledge
4 Park Square, Milton Park, Abingdon, Oxon OX14 4RN

and by Routledge
605 Third Avenue, New York, NY 10158

Routledge is an imprint of the Taylor & Francis Group, an informa business

For Product Safety Concerns and Information please contact our EU representative GPSR@taylorandfrancis.com. Taylor & Francis Verlag GmbH, Kaufingerstraße 24, 80331 München, Germany.

British Library Cataloguing-in-Publication Data
A catalogue record for this book is available from the British Library

ISBN: 978-0-8153-4697-5 (hbk)
ISBN: 978-0-8153-4698-2 (pbk)
ISBN: 978-1-351-16992-9 (ebk)

DOI: 10.4324/9781351169929

Typeset in Times New Roman
by KnowledgeWorks Global Ltd.

For my beautiful friends, Claire, my wife and Maddison-Grace, my daughter

And Pat, George, & Cheryl.

Born to Flow would not have come into being without your love, grace and presence.

Contents

This book is an idea.
An emergent property
of my life flowing.
It came slowly into being
and none of it may be true.
The energy you give it
and exploration of it
are what matters.

As you wonder
and wander
you may find it opens doors
go in, go deeper.
Move on with your questions!
Deeper toward things not yet known,
your tale will grow in its telling!*

Open mind, open heart.
Devotion to the beginner's mind,
an invitation to an exploration,
to the possibility of flow
in your life.
*Paraphrasing J. R. R. Tolkien
in the Introduction to *The Lord
of the Rings*

About the Forewords

The idea of asking a leader in elite sport and a leader from the world of commerce to contribute a foreword was driven by the notion that flow can be democratised across all fields of endeavour. I was fortunate enough to be able to ask two people whom I admire greatly, for their perspectives on leadership, Steve Borthwick and John Haughey, I am eternally grateful. Thank you.

Foreword

As I parked my car and turned off the engine, I paused before opening the door. The pause came from a small but noticeable amount of apprehension I held within me. Apprehension about what was going to happen in the next hour or so. Apprehension about stepping out of my comfort zone. The location I had driven to was not daunting in itself – it was a golf driving range.

The apprehension came from the fact that I am not a golfer. In fact, I've never had a desire to play golf. Early in my rugby career, I had taken a few lessons from a high-quality, experienced coach. But that was more because I felt I *should* learn to play golf, as many players did. After several lessons, without much improvement and not much enjoyment, I quickly reaffirmed that golf wasn't for me. And yet, here I was, sitting in my car at the driving range. No longer early in my playing career. Now, I was a few years older, early in my coaching career.

Yes, I was here to hit golf balls, but that wasn't the main purpose. I was here to expand my coaching skills. This was part of an experiential coaching education: Could I be coached to perform a skill I didn't have (and had never had)? And more importantly, what could I learn from the way my new coach approached the session, something I could bring into my own coaching practice?

There was another twist to this exercise. My coach was not a golf coach.

As I picked up the club and placed the ball on the tee, I tried to remember the tips I had been given years ago. I knew there was a specific order to them – I just couldn't remember what that order was.

There was a target for me to aim at. In those first few shots, I quickly looked up and tracked every ball I hit, hoping in vain it would go somewhere near the target. Each ball sailed, or sliced, or hooked, or bounced nowhere near where it was supposed to go. My expectations were that my swing would be ripped apart. But the expectations I held for this lesson were very quickly and silently dismissed.

In the hour that followed, there were no instructions about my grip, no feedback about my posture or stance, nothing about the angle of the club in my swing. In fact, there was a complete absence of any specific golf instruction. There were, however, some simple and consistent questions from my coach for me to consider.

I'm never going to be a golfer. I wouldn't even claim to *want* to be out on the course. In fact, nearly a decade later, I don't think I've ever visited a driving range again. But I remember that session. I remember walking in with so many thoughts about what I had to do, so many routines I was trying to recall. I remember how hitting the ball moved from a clunky, awkward experience to one of smoothness and even enjoyment.

After only a few minutes, I was getting the ball closer and closer to the target, closer than I could have imagined before the session. A few minutes further in, I didn't even need to see where the ball had landed. That had stopped being important. I was actually enjoying striking the ball. More than that, I was enjoying how simple the process now seemed. It felt easier, smoother. I was immersed in the process, immersed in the experience. Where the ball landed no longer mattered.

And remember: The coach in this session was not a golf coach.

Through a few simple questions, the coach helped me move from someone overwhelmed by too many cues to someone free of mental clutter. I was no longer getting in my own way.

That coach on the driving range that day was Cliff Kimber. At that point, I believe this book was only an idea. Cliff spoke to me about his intent to write a book on the topic of *flow*. And now, that idea has become reality.

Throughout my playing and coaching career, I've had countless conversations with elite sportspeople about their own performances and the performances of the teams they've been part of. Many of those conversations mirrored that moment on the driving range – too many thoughts, trying to force success, when in fact, they were just getting in their own way. I've also seen those same players and teams perform with such simplicity and joy that they made something incredibly tough look easy.

It's a feeling I've experienced as a player. In one of my early professional seasons, my team was going through a patch of indifferent results. Much like my golf swing, we were 'clunky'. But in the second half of that season, things changed. We won a tough, hard-fought game. Then another, more convincingly. What followed was a fantastic series of wins and a great finish to the season. That off-season, someone asked me how it felt to play in the team during that run. My answer: It felt *easy*. The game felt *smooth*. We were in a *groove*. We had *flow*.

At that time, my understanding of flow was rudimentary. I believed it was binary, you either had it or didn't. But that perspective shifted as my career progressed. As a player, I learned more about how I felt on any given day, and what I needed to do to get the best from myself. I learned to recognise the cues in those around me, too. In the best teams I was part of, we understood each other deeply – often without speaking. We could sense what a teammate needed to do to raise their performance.

Flow was no longer something you either had or didn't. It became more fluid, more empowering. I began to understand that we can recognise how we're feeling and adjust our behaviour and mindset in ways that help. Many of the best performers I've met excel at doing just that, recognising their feelings and responding intelligently.

No one *wants* to go through tough periods. But I've come to understand that without those challenges, our understanding doesn't grow. Without that friction, maybe we don't develop into who we're meant to become.

This book is for anyone striving for consistent high performance in any field. It's for those who want to learn more about themselves. It's for those who want to help others in their teams consistently deliver at a high level. It shows how *flow* is a natural state – a continuous one. It's always part of us on our journey, and we're all at different stages. For those of us in team environments, flow will feel different for each of us. But we can share the experiences, and the more we share, the deeper our understanding becomes.

This book reveals how flow is far from the binary concept many, including myself, have once believed. In fact, as Cliff explains, it couldn't be further from that. This is a book readers can return to again and again. Different parts will resonate more deeply at different times, depending on where you are on your journey.

While I left my golf game behind at that driving range years ago, I've carried forward the simplicity Cliff helped me discover that day. I still remember the smoothness. The enjoyment of being immersed in the process. The way flow developed through that lesson.

And I remember something Cliff has said to me many times – something that feels fitting to write here as you begin this book:

'Flow well'.

Steve Borthwick
England Head Coach, RFU

Foreword

Growing up, *flow* had always been something I associated with achieving a state of peak performance, the perfect assimilation of a person's ability to deliver flawlessly under extreme pressure. For me, this was invariably linked to sporting prowess, think Nadia Comăneci and her perfect 10s, Diego Maradona, the perfect 10, or Torvill and Dean and their unforgettable performance at the 1984 Olympics.

But as I got older, I began to experience my own 'flow' moments, albeit at a much less rarefied level, in the various sports and professional activities I took part in. That wondrous feeling of time slowing, of heightened sensory perception and perfect subconscious execution, though fleeting, was always intoxicating. So maybe, just maybe, if I could access it, *flow* wasn't something only reserved for the gods.

To be fair, I didn't give it much thought until many years later. Cliff was my executive coach as I prepared to take on more senior roles in my professional services career. At the time, he was at the beginning of his odyssey of putting his thoughts down on paper, thoughts that would eventually culminate in this book, *Born to Flow*.

During our sessions, we explored how I could eliminate some of the personal and professional 'frictions' I was experiencing, so I could operate at my maximum potential. This, in turn, would ensure that I could support my teams and those around me in helping *them* achieve their potential. As *flow* is not just an individual pursuit, it can be harnessed to deliver exceptional performance at a collective level too. I didn't realise it at the time, but I think I was one of Cliff's early case studies.

The central premise of Cliff's work, that *flow* is an innate, dynamic, complex psychological process that each of us, under the right conditions, can tap into is potentially profound. The possible positive implications for human endeavour, potential, and cooperation are vast.

Over the past decade, our personal and professional lives have suffered an unparalleled sensory overload. The borders between work and play have blurred, if not been erased, and technology has increasingly impacted our ability to focus for more than a few seconds. This evolutionary decline has had huge impacts on every walk of life and on our children's mental health. If we could begin to remove some of these cumulative frictions, maybe, just maybe, we could restore access to a 'lost' and innate process that we are, indeed, born to flow.

I recommend this book to anyone interested in exploring the achievement of peak performance and the potential paths to realising their and their team's true potential. *Born to Flow* is relevant irrespective of your field of endeavour and, given the times we live in today, it has never been timelier.

John Haughey
Former Vice-Chair and Global Life Sciences and
Health Care Consulting Leader at Deloitte

Part I

The Invitation

Chapter 1

A Droplet

This is a down-to-earth book, really; it isn't a grand intellectual theory. However, I believe it offers a new view of flow, as a gestalt experience, perhaps. A latent part of our make-up that comes to the fore is more than the sum total of our parts, an emergent property.

By analysing intellectual or academic papers on flow research, of which there have been some 2,622 or so published, Yongfa Zhang and Fei Wang's (2024) 'Developments and Trends in Flow Research over 40 Years: A Bibliometric Analysis Collections' offers the orthodoxy or canonical view of what flow is; you just need to use the all-knowing Google machine.

This book asks you to suspend your assumptions about what is theoretically 'known' and take on the radical responsibility for your own flow, be radically accountable for developing it, and chart your progress which will be iterative, experiential, experimental, and hopefully enjoyable.

And perhaps you will learn to accept flow, as the sum total of your being, of the latent flow expressing itself as you meet your 'best self' daily, but as Bruce Lee said, 'Honestly expressing yourself…it is very difficult to do.-. But to express oneself honestly, not lying to oneself…now that, my friend, is very hard to do' (Abridged quote) (Myszka et al., 2023).

A river takes care of itself, flowing back to the source. When it becomes cluttered with things that impede its flow, it becomes sluggish, overloaded with things that it doesn't need, over-complicated by interference from unwelcome interventions; it becomes a trickle of its former self, much like our mind. Our mental state is impacted in a similar way, and we must take care of ourselves.

References

Myszka, S., Yearby, T., & Davids, K. (2023). Being water: How key ideas from the practice of Bruce Lee align with contemporary theorizing in movement skill acquisition. *Sport, Education and Society*, *29*(4), 1–17. https://doi.org/10.1080/13573322.2022.2160701

Zhang, Y., & Wang, F. (2024). Developments and trends in flow research over 40 years: A bibliometric analysis. *Collabra: Psychology*, *10*(1), 1–17.

DOI: 10.4324/9781351169929-2

Chapter 2

Introduction
The Source

When a river is born, it begins a journey, flowing gently at first, but as it does so, it gradually starts to express its presence through the path it carves across the face of the earth on its journey towards the ocean – in much the same way that we humans leave the mark through our existence, for good or bad, real, or imagined, on people and on the planet.

And there are no straight rivers, in the same way there are no shortcuts to fulfilment or success or mastery; life is absent of linearity across time or space.

The river flows until it meets an obstruction, and then it flows over or around, it erodes and cuts beneath, or it is dammed. It is the friction and the obstacles that the river meets as it flows that give it shape, much as the friction we encounter in our lives shapes us and, how we react to that friction is key to us moving from surviving to thriving in our lives.

The river's only task is to flow, as it were, and to express itself as it does so, unless we, as an agent in the landscape, 'interfere'. As Alan Watts (2011) wrote,

> We do not hear nature boasting about being nature, nor water holding a conference on the technique of flowing. So much rhetoric would be wasted on those who have no use for it. The man who lives the Tao lives in the Tao, like a fish in water, if we try to teach the fish that water is physically compounded of two parts hydrogen and one part oxygen, the fish would laugh it's head off.

Water, its flow and precious nature, lends itself well to unpicking some of the beliefs that have unfolded around the work of Professor Mihaly Csikszentmihalyi, the renowned Hungarian psychologist, who recognised and named flow as a 'state' that humans can sometimes get into, and that flow is dependent on task and that happiness is dependent on the relative success in undertaking that task. This is, I think, fallacy and reification. For clarity, 'Reification is when an abstract concept comes to be seen as something concrete', as Lynn Waterhouse (2013), in Rethinking Autism, aptly describes it. The flow orthodoxy would also have it that a prerequisite set of circumstances needs to be in play for someone to achieve flow or move from a normative state into 'a flow state'. Notice, move into 'a' flow state, not 'the' flow state, as flow is, by all accounts, a subjective experience.

DOI: 10.4324/9781351169929-3

This is interesting, at one and the same time, a prerequisite number of things need to be in play for an individual to experience flow, which will be subjective because of their individual construing. It may well be different from all the flow states that ever existed, and yet for a person to experience flow, a requisite number of, mainly mental, processes need to be present. So, we will place a phenomenological lens across the ideas in *Born to Flow* and put you, the reader, at the centre of your flow experience, of your life; a focus on your experience and awareness around your flow rather than the *named* thing that flow has become.

Rick Rubin (2023) talks about 'context' in his wonderfully elusive and yet illuminating book *The Art of Creativity* and says something pertinent that speaks to the subjective context of our own flow experiences, and not least to the way that I will make the case for broadening the definition of flow beyond being a 'state'.

Rubin (2023) writes,

> When we don't have context, new ideas appear foreign or awkward. Sometimes the ideas that least match our expectations are the most innovative. By definition, revolutionary ideas have no context. They invent their own. When we initially experience the radically new, our first instinct might be to push it away and think, this is not for me. And sometimes it may not be.

What will be critical for the reader of *Born to Flow* is to firmly base themselves in their own context, balancing their flow experience only in a subjective way against the orthodoxy, as we will see, if comparison is the thief of joy, it may also be the enemy of flow when we are attempting to understand our own life experiences of it.

Csikszentmihalyi's hypothesis has an enduring appeal because it is axiomatic in its shape. I argue that flow is a subjective view of oneself at a given point in time and through time, and that Csikszentmihalyi's flow hypothesis is an extrapolated construct based on his extensive research and an interpretation that construes this change in mental state, as 'flow'. It could even be, as Gregory Bateson (2016) put it, an explanatory principle, 'something that is used to explain pretty much anything you don't understand'.

The challenge to this, is predicated on the notion that if flow is 'not' there and then 'is' there, what 'state' exists before and after *flow*. It also begs the question, is flow on a continuum? Further, if there is a flow potential, something must be lying dormant, something that might be deemed as a potential emergent property.

The axiomatic approach of *Born to Flow* will argue that flow is ever present, in much the same way that Professor Leroy Little Bear, would argue that all things are animate, because he has a holistic view of the motion and flux that is central to his cultural beliefs, and I will suggest that flow begins when we do and ends when we do, and in-between there are the ebbs and flows of a life lived, just as a river ebbs and flows from wellspring to ocean.

Writing *Born to Flow* gave me the opportunity to meet and talk with so many people who were gracious with their time and patient with my questions, and who are accomplished in their fields of endeavour. I hope that they will add flavour and perspective as we embark on our voyage down river, revealing, perhaps a different way for you to think about flow, your flow, and what you might achieve through developing it further, in much the same way we develop our thinking or philosophy of life, for example, the way we construct our mental map of the world we inhabit.

It is a fundamental law of physics that the less friction something encounters, the faster it will move. Yet, pragmatically we know, life is full of friction, both mental and physical, however one construes it, and in a strange way this is how we know we are in flow, if we are attentive to it. The things we rub up against, emotionally, physically, or psychologically, indicate how well we are flowing. One of the five laws of friction is an apt descriptor for this experience; friction depends upon the nature of the surfaces in contact.

Identify the friction in your life and you have the possibility of increasing flow. Let the friction overwhelm you and you may experience less and let's face it most friction occurs in our mind; at the very same place flow occurs – indeed the only place where flow occurs until it leaves the body as action or performance. And as Marcus Aurelius, Roman Emperor, A.D. 161–180 wrote, 'You have power over your mind – not outside events. Realize this, and you will find strength' (Aurelius, 1966).

When we come up against something that causes us psychological friction, it draws our attention away from the way we want to be in the world. And the only thing we have control over is our mindset; focussing on what we can control, rather than what we can't control because where attention goes, our energy flows. Friction is all around and ever present, the stuff of life. It is the mental model, the mindset adopted for dealing with friction that enables more flow in our lives, more enjoyment, fulfilment, and performance in our endeavours, that in some ways moves us from the hedonic to the eudaemonic.

For the originator of the flow hypothesis, Csikszentmihalyi, the frictions in his original model are 'boredom' and 'anxiety'. He postulates that these frictions are responsible for reducing our performance from optimal to suboptimal. This is partially why *Born to Flow* construes that 'flow' is a way of being and exists outside a dependency on task.

When we see someone living in flow, at their peak in sport perhaps, or delivering an extraordinary speech, or the craftsman, or someone simply pursuing life with flowfulness, we could also pay attention to the friction that could slow them down. In doing so, we notice how they flow through that experience NOT trying to avoid it, subjugate it, or deny it, but dealing with it in the moment and using it as an energy, as Michael Caine (2018) has said, 'use the difficulty' and by definition that is a mindset.

As an advanced Red2Blue performance under pressure coach, I might say that people in flow can be comfortable being uncomfortable and they are focussed, with intensity, on what they can control i.e., themselves. And usually associated with their endeavour, there is some purposefulness; some deep inner desire or motivation, or curiosity within their being, trying to express itself through flow, and, importantly, it is significant to them. Metaphorically 'letting go' of 'a task' immediately reduces friction and increases flow. A paradox perhaps, but in so suggesting, one unpicks at the myth of flow and the orthodoxy that perpetuates flow as task-related.

If you have had the experience of learning to drive, you will probably recognise some of the thoughts that ran through your head as you tried to get the car to move; seatbelt on, adjust mirrors, adjust seat, switch ignition, accelerator, brake, clutch, handbrake, indicators, steering wheel, and then the order or sequence of things to have the vehicle move.

What I found in enabling my daughter to drive was that the more she let go of trying, thinking, and calculating and focussed on the flow of things, the quicker the car moved. In subsequent 'drives', we decided to focus on two things that she would use to reflect on how a drive went; safe drive and flow drive, and they are not mutually exclusive. In the beginning, the focus was on safe drive and the scores *she* assigned were so weighted i.e., higher for task, lower for flow, the heavy lifting of conscious thinking, conscious incompetence. As the driving progressed and understanding was assimilated into her way of being when in the car, the flow level went up to reach parity with task score and as time went by the flow score overtook the task score and the level of enjoyment in moving from the 'task of driving' to the 'flow of driving', of being a driver, went up.

We see this in everyday occurrences, moving from conscious incompetence to unconscious competence, but rarely paying attention to the 'everyday' experience of flow. And I would suggest that paying attention to an unconscious competence i.e., bringing it to the front of your mind brings you closer to recognizing a flow experience. And often we do not ask why our conscious incompetence causes so much friction in our lives; in that moment we have the opportunity to smooth things out, reduce friction, and increase optimal performance in our way of being, in the world, and in our work, however we construe work.

When I first started, The Evolution Partnership, my coaching practice, I put some effort into having a home office in the garden. In reality, it was a place where I went to think and write, make client calls, skype friends around the world and read; it had many uses. From the very beginning it was called 'The Shed'; it even had a sign, 'SHED'. I didn't want that space to be constrained by the name, to be associated with only work. I wanted it to give freedom to the space to produce an optimal space for being creative. Even though my office is now upstairs in my house it's still called 'The Shed'; the sign is still on the door.

I suspect we don't investigate conscious incompetence for a couple of reasons: There is the assumption that over time we will get better, and also asking for feedback about our incompetence (we could ask for feedback about our potential too) increases the perception that we will also invite scrutiny and with that comes consequence.

Back to the river. If we consider the contours of our river and its meanderings, we cannot help but notice it is shaped by the limestone, sandstone, and different types of terrain that it encounters, and in forming the way it does, it creates havens where the fish can rest, where wildlife flourishes, as well as the superhighway rapids. But the flow in the river persists and as Bruce Lee was fond of saying to achieve optimum results, 'Be like water, my friend'.

Summary

In this chapter, we find:

- There are no straight rivers, in the same way there are no shortcuts to fulfilment or success; life is absent of linearity.
- The friction we encounter in our lives shapes us and how we react to that friction is key to us moving from survive to thrive in our lives.
- Water lends itself well to unpicking some of the beliefs that have unfolded around the work of Mihaly Csikszentmihalyi.
- Csikszentmihalyi was a renowned Hungarian psychologist, who recognised and named flow as a 'state' that we get into, and that flow is dependent on task/ activity, skill/challenge.
- Flow is, by all accounts, a subjective experience.
- 'When we don't have context, new ideas appear foreign or awkward' according to Rick Rubin.
- If there is a flow potential, something must be lying dormant; something that might be deemed as a potential emergent property.
- An explanatory principle by Gregory Bateson: 'something that is used to explain pretty much anything you don't understand'.
- Life is full of 'friction', and in a strange way this is how we know we are in flow. The things we 'rub up against', emotionally, physically, or psychologically indicate how well we are flowing.
- Identify the friction in life and then you have the possibility of increasing flow.
- Metaphorically 'letting go' of 'task' immediately reduces friction and increases flow.
- Paying attention to an unconscious competence i.e., bringing it to the front of your mind brings you closer to recognizing a flow experience.
- Bruce Lee said, 'Be like water, my friend'.

Exercise/Reflective Practice

1 Life is absent of linearity and yet we are often caught in the trap of thinking that one thing neatly follows another. As you reflect on the highs and lows of your life or career, the unexpected events, or the plot twists, where and how have you learnt the most?
2 If the friction we encounter during our lives helps shape us, can you identify what friction looks/feels/sounds like to you and do you have mindset strategies for overcoming the friction?
3 Do you reflect on how you receive new ideas? Do you have a beginner's mind as it were? Is Rick Rubin right in his assertion?

4 Does 'being like water' mean anything to you in your life experience and if not, could it? You can watch Lee explaining it in this excerpt: https://www.youtube.com/watch?v=cJMwBwFj5nQ

References

Aurelius, M. (1966). Meditations (M. Staniforth, Trans.). Penguin Classics, L140.

Bateson, G. (2016). *Metalogue 7: What is an instinct?* Posted on February 17, 2016 by Bateson for Business.

Caine, M. (2018). *Blowing the bloody doors off: And other lessons in life.* Hachette, UK.

Rubin, R. (2023). *The art of creativity.* Canongate Books Ltd.

Waterhouse, L. (2013). *Rethinking autism*: Variation and complexity. 1st ed. Academic Press.

Watts, A. (2011). *Tao: The watercourse way.* Souvenir Press.

Chapter 3

The Wellspring

The Abundant Source

This book has been gathering momentum for some time; the trickle of an idea started to become a stream, driven by two or three specific life events, but none more so than reading Csikszentmihalyi's seminal work, *Flow: The Psychology of Happiness* in 1992 and then coming back to it in 2000, and the birth of my daughter that same year. It happened again when I began my Masters in Coaching and Development at the University of Portsmouth, with faculty that included Sir John Whitmore, David Whitaker, OBE, (Order of the British Empire), and Sue Slocombe, OBE. I mention this because they were at the forefront of both executive coaching and elite performance in sport, and opened my heart and mind to how we develop potential in ourselves and others.

As I watched my daughter grow during her first few years, I found myself becoming more and more enveloped in the idea that there was another way to think about 'flow'. One that was as axiomatic as the first, but veered away from, what had become, the reification of the original thinking. And I also became more aware of my own way of being in the world, which was a constant and consistent ebb and flow, but always there was flow.

In 1998 I had been out on a mountain bike ride with a friend on the south downs of Sussex in the UK. We came to an incline, Whitbread Hollow, about 550 feet above sea level, and fairly steep, probably about a 1 in 10 slope at its steepest. And that's pretty much all I remember until I woke up about 45 minutes later, my life saved by a mate who knew my flow was ebbing away as I had swallowed my tongue and he had unblocked my airway; I was strapped to a spinal board. The area was difficult to gain access to and the paramedic told me he thought I had broken my back; I had no feeling chest down and that he had called for the rescue helicopter. I do remember the blush response, the flow of blood to my face felt searing, and the sheer embarrassment of the 'fuss' I was causing. I insisted I was 'only winded' and that I would be alright in a minute. The paramedic treated the comment with a subtle humour it deserved and replied, 'you lay there and be winded, I'll get the helicopter'.

My flow had been interrupted in a fairly dramatic kind of way. My mum and dad both saw me and expected the worst; my flow would be halted permanently, they were told I would leave hospital in one of two ways, probably – in a box or in

DOI: 10.4324/9781351169929-4

a wheelchair. In hospital I had all the equipment surrounding me of someone who has little or no feeling from the chest down, massive doses of morphine, mirrors around the bed so I didn't move but could see what was going on, and all the scans you could have, and excellent care from the NHS (National Health Service).

But, and it's a big but, I couldn't get people to listen to me; people talked at me, over me, around me and when they did talk to me, it was normally to try and reassure me in some way; the way people talk to people when they don't know or aren't sure what they should say. Friction, particularly psychological friction, was being generated. Other things have happened during my life, as they surely have in yours, some more dramatic than others, perhaps more of which later.

Another critical change for me was watching my daughter growing and becoming, moving from a quadruped to a biped, completely in flow. And it wasn't associated with task as such, it was coming from a place of being, of innate curiosity manifesting from innate potential into performance.

This book fills a void about what flow is or at least could be, and it is about its democratization; it enables you to own it because you were born to flow.

Reference

Csikszentmihalyi, M. (1992). *Flow: The psychology of happiness*. Rider & Co.

Chapter 4

Scene Setting
Tributary

When people talk of flow today, there seems to be a binary conclusion to be drawn; put simply, you are either in flow or you are not.

Since flow entered the consciousness, first as 'Flow – The Psychology of Happiness' and then much more in relation to performance in 'Flow – The Psychology of Optimal Performance', it would appear that most people have accepted the canonical view that flow is a 'state' to get into. This has been somewhat perpetuated by commentators and pundits, especially regarding sport and the arts. The hypothesis of 'in flow' or 'not in flow' has been accepted as a truth.

Born to Flow challenges the orthodox view and offers a notion as powerful, if not more so, more axiomatic, as stated, you are **born to flow**. My journey began in earnest, with the pure example of a baby, my daughter, as mentioned, transitioning from a quadruped to a biped and in doing so fulfilling all of the subjective criteria, set out below, offered up by the orthodoxy as a prerequisite for 'getting into the flow state' or 'reaching the flow state'. And yet I noticed something emerging that points to flow as a way of being.

The eight characteristics of Csikszentmilayi's flow are

1 Complete concentration on the task.
2 Clarity of goals and reward in mind and immediate feedback.
3 Transformation of time (speeding up/slowing down).
4 The experience is intrinsically rewarding.
5 Effortlessness and ease.
6 There is a balance between challenge and skills.
7 Actions and awareness are merged, losing self-conscious rumination.
8 There is a feeling of control over the task.

Rebuttal of the flow task hypothesis:

1 Baby learning to crawl.
2 Evolutionary desire to stand; clear goal.
3 Time is a subjective construct and appears to change as we age generally.

DOI: 10.4324/9781351169929-5

4 Evolutionary desire rewards; we are hardwired to reward ourselves when we learn something of meaning.
5 Little concept of effortless or ease and yet needs to move (intrinsic motive).
6 From quadruped to biped fulfils this; a baby consistently, constantly up-skills.
7 A baby is lost in 'being' and actions and awareness merge in transition.
8 Humans desire control over their lives and yet it is mostly illusory.

And so, we can see the faintest glimmer that the notion, born to flow, proposes, takes the emphasis away from 'task', and places it firmly in 'being'. As George Kelly, father of personal construct theory (PCT or PCP) suggests, we are 'form in motion', (Kelly, 2003) and that motion is best when flow is recognised as a key component of being, not the 'task'.

When you choose to trust in the power of flow as a fundamental part of your make-up, like flight or fight, for example, which is mainly an unconscious response, you look at flow through a different lens and in much the same way that astronomers look to the sky through telescopes or scientists use a microscope to pull things closer. By observing the flow that exists in your life now, you can pull it into your way of being, not for fleeting seconds, or years, but for the rest of your life, as Marcus Aurelius wrote in his meditations (Barnett, 1976), as if talking of flow, 'Look well into thyself; there is a source of strength which will always spring up if thou will always look'.

Born to Flow covers a lot of ground, the notion being that flow is informed by, and informs, so much of who we are and how we express ourselves. This is perhaps more relevant in a world that is geared, deliberately or not, to disrupt flow, to the extent we forget it is always at hand, as we will see.

Frances Crick, a scientist, and Nobel Laureate, responsible for much of the work on the structure of DNA, proposed that evolution had enabled the brain to sieve out what was useful and what was to be disregarded.

We have some inbuilt help in maintaining our attentiveness to things we are interested in. The soft machine is constantly sieving. If we are interested in our flow and maintaining it, the brain is on hand to help us do so, to screen out friction and disruption where it is not useful.

The corollary, of course, is that our brains evolved in very different circumstances and whilst humans have proved themselves the most adaptable of creatures, it may well be that today's society and our deep intersection of human beings with technology weigh heavily against an organ that is still making its way into the 18th century. Our thinking can get in the way and Steven Pinker (1997) goes further when he writes in *How the Mind Works*, 'the modern mind is adapted to the stone age, not the computer age'. The sheer mass of data that bombards us daily simply could not have been imagined 50 years ago. As an example of the pace tech is moving at, in 2019, more photographs were taken in the first quarter of that year than ever before, since the invention of photography; in a mere 90 days.

I think living *with* flow enriches the experience of life and allows access to a different way of attending to oneself and the world at large. By definition, paying attention to your flow is to pay attention to your latent potential and by doing that, you bring the world closer to your best self, as potential is nothing if it doesn't leave the body as action.

I think there is a corollary to that, flow is to express potential in such a way that all of oneself understands it at some level. Perhaps, this manifests for you, as a feeling, a deeper understanding, intuition, or a psychic effortlessness, and the notion that I put before you informs everything that follows, that is, a person is born to flow and in remembering and recognising this, they can have more control over the way they experience and perform in the world.

And it should be noted that remembering is an excellent way to reconnect back into your ever-present flow in a meaningful and significant way. Again, life is the task, and that might appear quite a stoic sentiment, but a stoic might argue that the stuff we normally busy ourselves with is agnostic to our fulfilment i.e., the stuff we do doesn't care if we do it or not.

Born to Flow: A Fundamental Postulate

'A person is born to flow and in remembering that, an individual can influence the course of their life path. Only through interaction does a person's ability to flow well emerge'.

Corollaries:

1 A person has the potential to remember that they are born 'in' and 'to' flow.
2 A person's ability to remember that they were born 'in' or 'to' flow is dependent on the way that they start to, and are educated to, construe their world.
3 A person's construing of flow will be subjective.
4 A person's ability to flow may be conditional on the 'stressors' that they construe exist in their lives and may be limited by their environment if they do not curate it, and a flow mind shift.

Are we born to flow emerged from a simple question, 'If flow is a state to get into, what state are we in when we are not in flow?'. If there is no flow in a river, stagnation can quickly cause deterioration in the river's capacity to sustain life. We can also see this in the deterioration of neural plasticity when something goes wrong with someone's health. And another question effortlessly follows the first, 'where is flow if not within us?'. The flow canon is more or less adamant that the perfect storm of task, capacity, and capability/challenge and skills, emerging at the right time produces flow.

The idea that only under certain circumstances, we 'enter' a state that enables us to experience or perform at a level we hadn't previously reached, seemed absurd and illogical to me as I watched my daughter reaching, unbidden, for the stars by anything other than her innate being and curiosity. It seemed to rule out subjective experience, context, intent, and expression as a human being.

As Csikszentmihalyi himself conceded, 'In outlining the flow model the author states that the objective nature of the activity itself is not enough to characterise a person being in "flow"' (Csikszentmihalyi, 2013). And as Lynn Barnett (1976, p. 83) notes, 'in other words the subjective evaluation of the individual must be considered'.

What if flow is ever present, if we could remember that it is part of our make-up, that we have inherent capabilities and we are predisposed to flow and what if we could regulate our flow state, from low flow to high flow, perhaps? What might our lives be like then? What if we expressed our life through flow, built our lives around it because it is always there?

Flow seems to be a thing that lives in the past tense, that is, you hear people talking about having been in flow, but rarely, if at all, hear people say they are in flow or better still they are in flow and going to *increase* their flow intensity.

There are always exceptions and Michael Kopech, a major league baseball player for the Chicago White Sox, formerly of the Boston Red Sox, was one. In 2016 in an article in the Chicago Tribune by Dan Weiderer, Kopech talked about his fascination with meditation, being in the 'now', his watch only had one time, 'NOW' on the dial, and at the time Weiderer wrote, 'His (Kopech) search for the "flow state" continues. "When I get rolling", Kopech says, "that's my flow state. I find a state of mind where I feel like there's nothing I can do wrong. It's almost an out-of-body experience. I feel like I'm watching myself pitch". What's interesting is that Kopech goes onto say, 'later in the article, It's living in the present with a focus on the future'.

Weiderer (2016) further writes,

Kopech chuckles and apologizes for 'sounding like some crazy guru'. But he can't help his growing fascination with learning how to be truly mindful. 'It's understanding the journey', he says. 'I'm a guy who is going to put everything I have into right now, but with attention on where I'm going'.

That is, he's flowing into the future.

For a state to exist that we only realise we were in, post hoc, seems counter to what we are as human beings – we watched the birds in the sky and we worked out how to do it, although not with the birds their grace, we've looked at, and in some cultures worshipped the moon since the dawn of time and we eventually got there, we've worked out calculus and talked philosophy, we've climbed mountains and trained our minds and bodies to do incredible things, but still, rarely do we hear someone say, 'today I am going to enjoy my flow'.

And we rarely hear people say that they are going to be 'in the zone', again it's always after the event, as if something other-worldly conspired to get them there, which is strange because the phrase has its roots in the sci-fi TV series of the 1950s and 1960s called, 'The Twilight Zone'. The great tennis player, Arthur Ashe coined the phrase in 1973 or 1974 after a match with Bjorn Borg, widely considered to be one of the greatest tennis players of all time. https://quoteinvestigator.com/2016/09/16/zone/.

Mark Wilson, a professor in psychology, with an applied and theoretical interest in understanding the cognitive and emotional processes that underpin skill acquisition and performance under pressure, said when we met,

> I think the problem is there's an issue with definition, because if you don't know what something is, or what you name it, it's cloudy. And you can't test it, or you can't rate it because you can be rating anything. So, what is it you're measuring when you're measuring flow? Is it just absorption? It doesn't matter what it is, if you perform better. And if you rate something after you've done something, are you more likely to go, if you did well, 'Yes, I was in flow'. I think that's the biggest issue with flow research.

Wilson further said,

> So if you've performed well, you're likely to go, oh, yeah, I got everything right. That was awesome. And if you've performed badly, you're more likely to go, I just wasn't quite there. And I think there's some of the difficulties from a research perspective in terms of testing something like flow.

We know we are going to eat, sleep, work, and repeat. We know we are going to have good days and great days, and the inevitable bad day when you are blindsided by something and the only thing you have control over is your mind-set and mental state. We prepare for meetings and tournaments, for war and for peace, we meditate, we study, we educate and contemplate, we build, and we plan but we seem not to acknowledge that we flow, that we can own it and it's not dependent on the twilight zone.

And as Pinker writes in the preface to *How the Mind Works*,

> The linguist Noam Chomsky once suggested that our ignorance can be divided into problems and mysteries. When we face a problem, we may not know its solution, but we have insight, increasing knowledge, and an inkling of what we are looking for. When we face a mystery, however, we can only stare in wonder and bewilderment, not knowing what an explanation would even look like.
>
> (Pinker, 1997)

And perhaps that's part of the problem, that flow is perhaps a mystery, and like all good mysteries, it might wait through millennia of 'wondering', perhaps until science breaks through, or that consciousness, the other great mystery of the brain, breaks out of its shell to reveal itself and flow to us.

'Flow' had currency long before it was appropriated as a psychological state. Construing 'flow' in the only way that the current optimal performance orthodoxy does, may be preventing the true benefits and nature of a flow construct from enabling people, through their own construing of flow, to make great gains in their performance, fulfilment in life, and wellbeing. 'Your skin does not separate you from the world. It's a bridge through which the external world flows into you. And you flow into it' as Alan Wilson Watts reminds us.

Optimal experience is a construing of 'peak' performance and whilst that holds true for the very elite in sport, just the acknowledgement that you are born to flow opens up possibilities that may never have been considered as a way of increasing flow or performance.

Performance, enjoyment, learning, identity, and desire, for example, of a person to live a more productive and fulfilled life expands through their own construing of flow; it is no longer dependent on another's interpretation or criteria or on a task an individual might be set.

Flow is an expression of a life lived in the moment and reaches back into our history to give us understanding of our place and abilities, and also, critically, reaches out into the future where people could flourish; ideas should be unfettered by lack of imagination or received wisdom and where business and sports performance can truly enable a different construing of what might be possible when you flow. In diagram 4.1, Flow in the present moment we can see the elements of past, future and now coming together in flow.

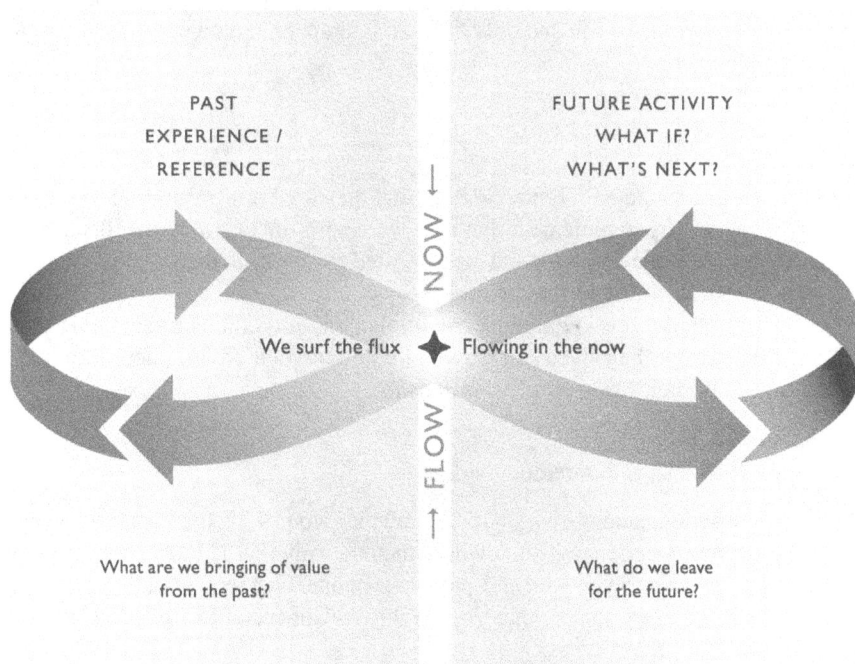

PAST
EXPERIENCE /
REFERENCE

FUTURE ACTIVITY
WHAT IF?
WHAT'S NEXT?

NOW

We surf the flux   Flowing in the now

FLOW

What are we bringing of value
from the past?

What do we leave
for the future?

Born to Flow®

Figure 4.1 Flow in the present moment

Summary

In this chapter, we see and discover:

- A child standing fulfils all of the prerequisite characteristics of getting into 'flow' as per the flow orthodoxy, but the child has no idea what flow is. The child is simply 'being'.
- The idea of getting 'into flow' has undergone reification. It has somehow moved from the subjective to the objective, and no one, except you, can tell you whether you are flowing or not. And having to 'get into the flow state' could be considered a barrier to actually deepening your flow.
- The subjective evaluation of what an individual considers 'flow' must be considered and as Shannon L. Alder states, 'One of the greatest regrets in life is being what others would want you to be, rather than being yourself'.
- Csikszentmihalyi concedes, 'In outlining the flow model the author states that the objective nature of the activity itself is not enough to characterize a person being in "flow"'.
- The modern world has an unparalleled capacity to disrupt flow, and this requires attention.
- 'A person is born to flow and in remembering that, an individual can influence the trajectory of their life and only through interaction does a person's ability to flow well emerge'.

  Corollaries

- A person has the potential to remember that they are born 'in' and 'to' flow.
- A person's ability to remember that they were born 'in' or 'to' flow is dependent on the way that they start to, and are educated to, construe their world.
- A person's construing of flow will be Subjective.
- A person's ability to flow may be conditional based on the 'stressors' that they construe exist in their lives and may be limited by their environment if they do not curate it (their life) and a flow mindshift.

Exercise/Reflective Practice

1 If you are serious about living with and owning your flow, then you could capture how you experience it somewhere in some way that is interesting, significant, and relevant to you – on an I-pad, your phone, on paper, or perhaps a voice recording. I suggest this so that you might remember not to forget where you start and how you progress.
2 Notice the way you think people may be flowing (or not) whilst remembering you will be seeing their flow from your reality.
3 Reflect on whether flow is a problem to be solved or a mystery to be wondered at, curious about, and enjoyed through your own flourishing.

References

Barnett, L. (1976). Play and Intrinsic Rewards: a Reply To Csikszentmihalyi. *Journal of Humanistic Psychology, 16*(3), 83–87. https://doi.org/10.1177/002216787601600312 (Original work published 1976)

Csikszentmihalyi, M. (2013). *Flow: The psychology of happiness*. Penguin Random House.

Wiederer, D. (2016). Chicago Tribune online. https://digitaledition.chicagotribune.com/tribune/article_popover.aspx?guid=835ad426-079a-4888-95ff-9034246016e1 (accessed 1st june 2018)

Pinker, S. (1997). *How the mind works*. W.W. Norton.

Chapter 5

It Depends

Confluence

How you will benefit from the Born to Flow hypothesis and what you do with the results of your exploration of flow, will very much depend on whether you think of 'flow' as a 'state' to get into, or as I have revisited it, as 'a dynamic, complex, psychological process'.

The orthodoxy surrounding flow is very much one that it is a 'state' one gets into and is very much the result of the way that it was studied and developed by Csikszentmihalyi, and although the contribution he made to positive psychology cannot be underestimated or disputed, I think flow was, and still is, defined too narrowly and, as such there is room to redefine the way people look at it as an experience of life to be explored so that you might come closer to your better self.

As a social psychologist, his interpretation of his research and the emergent hypothesis that flow, as a state to get into, is not surprising, but as such it has become dogma, and rarely disputed, almost all research since the original work tends to look at the idea of flow in that way, through the 'state' lens. And flow has become one of the mimetic parasites that Csikszentmihalyi disliked so much when he wrote about the possibility of the evolving self; it has crept into consciousness and perhaps restricted other possible interpretations of flow.

I have deep gratitude that on my flow journey of writing Born to Flow, I have met some truly remarkable athletes, coaches, thinkers, doers, musicians, and amongst others, sports psychologists, one of whom is Professor Dave Collins, who was generous with his time and brutal in his criticism and encouragement, in equal measure, and I deeply appreciated both.

Dave uses a phrase that I love, 'it depends' and so entrenched in his thinking is this idea that he co-authored an excellent paper on it (Collins et al., 2022). Because if 'context is King', then 'It depends' surely sits alongside as Queen. I have found that in my work, just the phrase, 'it depends', when confronted with an issue, problem, or opportunity, gives access to a range of thinking that might stay contextually hidden. So, it is with Born to Flow, what you get from the book depends; it depends on your biology, your psychological well-being, your self-concept, your environment, your social circumstances, and the impact of technology on your life, and the context you are aiming to develop your flow in, amongst other things.

DOI: 10.4324/9781351169929-6

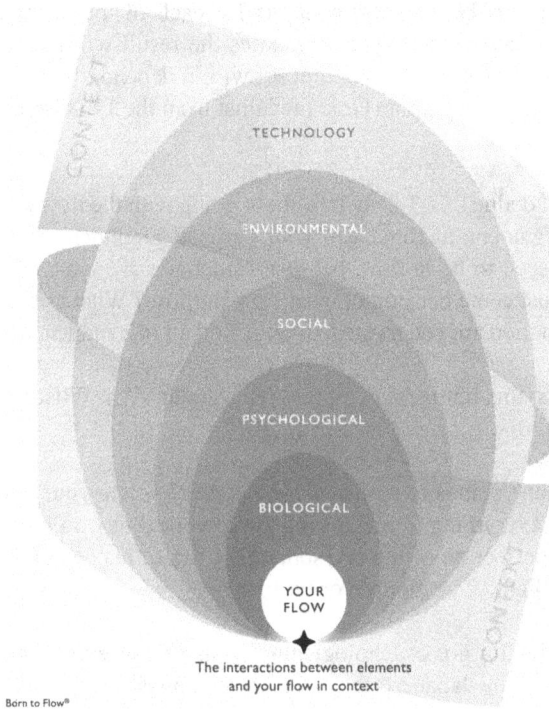

Figure 5.1 The flow intersection

In Figure 5.1, you can see the intersection of what I think are key elements for us as bio-psycho-social beings and where they intersect is probably the most important point. This is where the many interactions between each of the elements can occur. It is not linear, there is no import in the size of the circles, they are just representative of the potential combinations that exist, for example, your biology may be monitored by a piece of readily accessible med-tech like an Apple watch or a Fitbit, they intersect at the bottom. Or your sense of how you self-represent and your psychological representation to the world may be heavily influenced by your tribe or the environment you live in. Thus, this figure represents where these elements intersect and interact and that they anchor into your flow potentiality.

This diagrammatical representation of the key elements in your life enables you to examine where, when, and how you might meet your best self, and develop your flow growth. As Charles Hazlehurst, the composer puts it, (in flow) 'Everything elegantly connects up', and I think this is possible, but it depends.

Alignment is a key issue when it comes to building on your flow, on making the most of what is available to you as a resource. You cannot integrate what isn't aligned and you must align the differentiated elements as best you can, so that they meet within the essence of your being.

There will always be different contexts for each of the elements and where, when, and how they interact, and sometimes the result will not be conducive to your best flow experience and sometimes it will, it depends.

David Hemery, the Olympian Gold medallist from the 1968 Mexico games, says this,

> How would I define flow? They talk about going with the flow don't they, I think it's about alignment, alignment of your purpose, alignment of your intention, I think it's needed to be in flow, because sometimes if I have been out of alignment, but I just come back onto, what's the purpose? What are you trying to do? What contribution are you trying to make? And all of a sudden, the clarity comes.

In some ways, this reminds me of the Zen scholar, Alan Wilson Watts, when he said,

> In every art one comes to realise there is a point where your will is exhausted, you've tried everything to make something work & it won't work, and then to achieve the perfection of the art, something has to happen of itself, which we variously call grace, inspiration or tariki.

The idea of letting go, psychologically, so as to cause an alignment perhaps. Tariki or Jiriki is the Japanese term for 'other power' or 'outside help' and for achievement through one's own effort. So, raising our awareness about the way these elements impact and the power they have when aligned, might enable our flow experience, it depends.

Summary

- How you benefit from the Born to Flow hypothesis will depend, largely on whether you think of 'flow' as a 'state' to get into, or as I have defined it, as 'a dynamic, complex, psychological process'.
- Flow is an experience of life to be explored so that you might come closer to your best self.
- Flow could be considered to have become a mimetic parasite.
- Dave Collins is a world-renowned professor of sports psychology, but his knowledge and insight largely inform what many of us already know across many domains and his phrase, 'it depends', will help you find a place for your construing of flow.
- If 'context is King', then 'It depends' surely sits alongside as Queen.
- The key elements that impact our flow are bio-psycho-social- environmental-tech as in Figure 5.1 and it is the interaction of these with our flow process that can take us into flow deeper or reduce its impact through our lives.
- Charles Hazlehurst, the composer, said, in flow 'Everything elegantly connects up.'

- You cannot integrate what isn't aligned and you must align the differentiated elements as best you can, so that they meet within the essence of your flow. The elements' interactions are as important to your flow as the elements themselves.
- Understanding and aligning the biological, psychological, environmental, social, and technological aspects of your life in context are key to facilitating more flow in your life.

Exercise/Reflective Practice

1 Consider each of the elements in Figure 5.1. What is the first thought you have when you say each word?
2 How does each one rise in your conscious mind when you think about it?
3 How do you construe each element interacting with each other element?
4 Do think about those interactions often?
5 If you consider the elements interacting, does it raise the prospect of a new level of complexity in your life that you have not considered before?
6 In raising your awareness to think deliberately about the elements and their interactions, do you have to rethink your relationship with them as a whole or individually, for example?
7 Do you consciously try to align the elements to give best possible outcomes to your life and from a dynamic, complex, psychological process, do you get closer to understanding you were born to flow?

Highlights and Insights from the Interview with Ann Daniels, Polar Explorer, on the Experience of Flow

- (In flow) 'I start to breathe differently, I start to concentrate, I start to think. Everything else goes out of my "everyday" thinking'.
- 'I feel differently. And I feel more heightened and aware of things around me. And what's going on. I pay more attention'.
- 'I'm performing differently (in flow) because it matters'.
- 'Flow for me is about my energy, my awareness, my ability to **not** give in to the difficulties that come to us at all times and in every aspect of our lives'.
- 'Holding back. That's not flow'.
- 'I think other people can affect your flow. I don't think of my flow is in terms of other people's performance, but how I might deal with that performance. I think it does affect my flow. And I can allow it, or I cannot allow it. It can heighten my flow because I could help them be better and it might make me flow better if they're not performing well. If they're performing well, it might heighten (my flow) because we can go together, or it can drag me back. And I think the difference for me as to whether it would bring me back or heighten me, is whether I think they're not giving their all, I would hope I'm the type of person that would always try and help and always have sympathy and always go into a good flow and bring them with me'.

- 'Like it's a great state to get into (flow). I think it gives you a sense of being the best that you can be yourself. Not better than other people, but the best of yourself, and that is a good feeling. And I think that's why if you say, if you're in it, or you can help somebody else to get in it, and I think it's something that can perpetuate, and you can build on it and you can be better, the best of yourself'.
- (To flow) 'I think there's lots of contributing factors, you know, your family, you know if you have a great support system, then I think that does contribute to your ability to be in flow. I think you have a bad support system that can also contribute if you've got that mindset'.
- (On other contributing factors to Ann's flow) 'If I'm doing exercise and I'm eating and I'm, you know, outdoors, and I'm in sunshine, then all that feeds into me and my psyche and helps me to flow. So, I do, and the healthier that I am, the more that I perform and if you're strong physically, it helps you mentally'.
- 'I do think that it's (flow) this part of us, there is a natural flow and the barriers that we learn stop us. But then I think that there is a bit more preternatural that, you know, sometimes I have a sixth sense. And that's just weird. But it's there. I think that about flow, strangely, it's like some people can work on it, and it comes into them. And it's special'.

Reference

Collins, D., Taylor, J., Ashford, M., & Collins, L. (2022). It depends. Coaching – The most fundamental, simple and complex principle or a mere copout?. *Sports Coaching Review*, 1–21. https://doi.org/10.1080/21640629.2022.2154189

Chapter 6

Flow

Tributary

We are trying to fill the void left by dogmatic reification that what we are told is right or the truth of 'flow' and that has buried it ever deeper in a mystique over the last five decades. The prescriptive nature of what constitutes a person achieving the 'flow state' has continued to set flow up as something that is not within us.

Whilst Csikszentmihalyi (2013) states in the introduction to the 1992 edition of *Flow: The Psychology of Happiness*, 'This book summarises, for the general audience, decades of research on the positive aspects of human experience – joy, creativity, the process of total involvement with life I call flow'.

By his own admission in his TED talk in 2004, 'flow' was the word used at various stages by participants during interviews, subjectively; by definition the word suited the experience and henceforth used as an objective descriptor for an aspect of the human experience, that is unique to each individual. The map is not the territory and the word, is not the thing, to reference Korzybski (1931) and as the Zen scholar, Alan Watts suggested in a lecture in the -1960s, 'the menu is not the meal'.

Flow has been codified, and in a way that perhaps perpetuates the myth that prerequisites are required to experience it and in truth the only prerequisite might be that you are alive. In a conversation in 2017 with Eddie Jones, former England and Australia Head rugby coach and currently Japan head coach, when I spoke with him about Born to Flow, he asked if there were any absolutes, my reply was exactly as I have stated previously, 'You have to be alive to it'.

Given that the current view of flow orthodoxy is axiomatic and subjective, then I follow in that tradition, but it is objective inasmuch as it leaves the reader to determine their flow experience and not tell them what constitutes it. Your awareness and experience of how you feel in flow, what you construe it to be, the difference the experience makes in your life, are the only beautiful things that matter.

When one takes time to stop and consider the proposition, as I have done over the last two decades or so, the people that I work with, recognise in the statement, 'we are born to flow', a simple truth, if we are not flowing we are stagnating, becoming atrophied, and at that moment two things are clear, stagnation is followed by death and flow increases our experience of the world.

And Professor Luc Steels and Peter Wellen (2007) state in their paper, 'Scaffolding Language Using the Autotelic Principle', an individual seeking the

DOI: 10.4324/9781351169929-7

flow experience is always 'on the move'. And as George Kelly (2003), father of personal construct theory, proposes, we are 'beings in motion'. If so, we must be in some kind of flow, by definition.

The original 'flow' diagram also perpetuated the myth that 'up' or high in challenge or skills is always the best direction of travel; the original flow channel goes up from bottom left to top right on a double axis graph, along the horizontal, challenge, and on the vertical axis, skills.

I believe that to go 'forwards' is probably more representative of what people actually want and experience in their lives. Water seldom flows uphill without requiring enormous energy to enable it. So the idea that representing flow as a bottom to top trajectory is purely metaphorical, whereas we are actually going forwards into our future.

Going forwards in life, to stand and move forwards, learning to increase your flow, to survive and thrive on your own terms, maximising the time you are attentive to and using your flow – all this shows a more sustainable way of thinking about movement in life, rather than the ever-present demand that all things representing direction should be 'up' focussed.

In *Born to Flow* I have termed friction, those things that can impede flow, what appears as 'boredom' and 'anxiety', in the original diagram, but as we will discover 'friction' comes in many forms, and in one of them it helps formula 1 cars go faster and flow simultaneously: The science of aerodynamics, downforce, and grip. Figure 6.1 shows the original representation of the flow channel, which excludes you, the reader, from the frame.

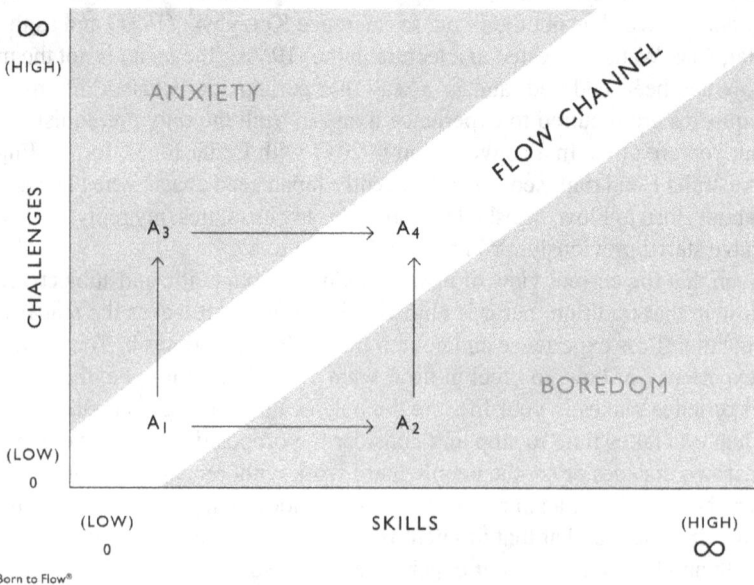

Born to Flow®

Figure 6.1 Csikszentmihalyi's original flow diagram

In the figure, 'A' represents Alex, a tennis player at four periods in time, the hypothesis being that boredom will draw him out of flow, as will anxiety, but the desire for growth of skills and the need to match the challenge through growth will eventually lead him back into flow (Csikszentmihalyi, 2013).

But it is hard to understand how equally matched challenge and skills increase our capability or capacity in situations that require an adaptive mindset if they are always balanced.

I have sometimes found my growth and flow come through my skills being just slightly underweight. So I'm stretched, which could cause me some anxiety, and I've also found that my flow increases exponentially in such circumstances. I have developed a way to be comfortable with being uncomfortable, which allows me to learn in flow, and I also understand that performance, enjoyment, and learning are inextricably linked to our being as well as our doing.

Figure 6.1 perpetuates the idea that flow is a state you are either in or not, rather than a deep examination of your innate flow and using it to grow through anxiety or boredom, to be assiduous in using that adaptive streak to meet your better self. Elite athletes and special forces consistently face repetition of tasks but they know that repetition is a step on the path, and controlling their attitude through a highly developed mindset is the only way forward.

Csikszentmihalyi suggests,

> An autotelic person needs few material possessions and little entertainment, comfort, power, or fame because so much of what he or she does is already rewarding. Because such persons experience flow in work, in family life, when interacting with people, when eating, even when alone with nothing to do, they depend less on external rewards that keep others motivated to go on with a life of routines. They are more autonomous and independent because they cannot be as easily manipulated with threats or rewards from the outside. At the same time, they are more involved with everything around them because they are fully immersed in the current of life.
>
> (Csikszentmihalyi & Csikszentmihalyi, 1990)

Again, there is a deep connection with the stoic approach to life in this paragraph.

Summary

In 'Flow', we see and discover:

- Csikszentmihalyi appropriated the word 'flow' and henceforth it became used as an *objective descriptor*.
- Flow has been codified, and in a way that perpetuates the myth that prerequisites are required to experience flow outside of being.
- If we are not flowing, we are stagnating, growth is unlikely.
- The orthodoxy perpetuates the idea that flow is a state you are either in or not.

- Born to flow suggests that for most people going forwards into a future they are actively creating is more representative than always trying to go 'up', unless one considers that self-actualisation is an intrinsic part of that journey, then Maslow's hierarchy of needs might be right.

Exercise/Reflective Practice

1 Consider if, on waking, how you feel flow. Perhaps the remnants of a flow dream or perhaps how sleep has enabled recovery from a day at the gym. Decide how and what you are measuring when feeling and thinking about the flow you wake to. Use something to record your thoughts and feelings. The formalisation of your everyday flow experience will help you build your own flow playbook and strengthen your relationship with your flow.
2 Here I introduce you to a confidence builder, developed specifically to encourage you to think about flow and there is a flow to the sequence: Clarity, simplicity, consistency, constancy, meaningful, significant = confidence. We can break that sequence down to give it meaning.

- Do you have clarity on the mission for the flow measurement?
- Breaking it down into simple steps will help.
- Being consistent is absolutely key (remember Bill Walsh, 'the challenge with consistency is being consistent' [Walsh et al., 2009]) but it pays benefits.
- Is there a constancy with the way you turn up to the day, each day, every day. Have you made this a campaign?
- Have you made this meaningful to your routine and what you will achieve by following through on continuing to feel you were born to flow?
- Is there significance to expressing your flow in the way that you turn up for the day?
- At the end of this sequence, you will feel more confident about the nature of being born to flow and you will build reserves in the same way people build mental toughness or resilience. Waking the following day with an open mind, be ready to continue the engagement with your flow.

References

Csikszentmihalyi, M. (2013). *Flow: The psychology of happiness*. Penguin Random House.
Csikszentmihalyi, M., & Csikszentmihalyi, M. (1990). *Flow: The psychology of optimal experience* (Vol. 1990, p. 1). Harper & Row.
Kelly, G. (2003). *The psychology of personal constructs: Volume two: Clinical diagnosis and psychotherapy*. Routledge.
Korzybski, A. "A non-Aristotelian system and its necessity for rigour in mathematics and physics," December 28, 1931. Reprinted in *Science and Sanity*, pp. 747–761. Institute of General Semantics
Steels, L., & Wellens, P. (2007, April). Scaffolding language emergence using the autotelic principle. In 2007 IEEE Symposium on Artificial Life (pp. 325–332). IEEE.
Walsh, B., Jamison, S., & Walsh, C. (2009). *The score takes care of itself: My philosophy of leadership*. Penguin.

Chapter 7

The Notion of Born to Flow

Tributary

Conceivably one of the most wonderful things that we can witness is a baby or small child, totally engaged in learning through play. This is possibly a human universal as described by Donald F. Brown (2004) when he refers to 'childcare' and 'play to perfect skills'.

Or those moments when a child starts learning to walk, reaching upwards to what, one might arguably say, is their evolutionary birth right. After a few tentative steps, they show a smile and an excitement. And then the inevitable tumble, tears, laughter, or confusion arises, but being left to their own devices, the child will take such setbacks in their stride, right themselves, and set off again until eventually they are eventually walking, increasing in confidence, with literally a new perspective of the world.

One element of what we are seeing in moments such as these is a being 'in flow' and as George Kelly says, a being in motion, not a body. Perhaps existing in flow is a part of our evolutionary predisposition to movement and growth, to move on from merely crawling to standing and from surviving to thriving, and if flow enables anything as you increase it, it is the capability to thrive. In general terms, a baby will walk because the call to be upright is so strong that the baby can no longer crawl.

But if at the moment of the child's first stumble someone intervenes, then they could disrupt the child's flow permanently, and a long shadow may be cast over the child's progress, as it slips unknowingly from being completely flowing in its own world, into one where that overwhelming impulse to stand is usurped by an overwhelming need to please because of the 'feedback' they are receiving.

When I shared this notion with Steve Borthwick, former England rugby captain, then Head Coach at Leicester Tigers, now England Head Coach, he added, 'and to prove'. This is an important and interesting distinction and an important addition to the thinking and our conversation necessarily leads to, 'prove to whom?' to prove to oneself, to the observer, or simply to prove that the child is reaching some level of readiness to join a wider community.

In the case of Jane (not their real name), former CEO of a UK charity, she is very clear it was to 'prove' to others. Having been in a wheelchair since birth and then institutionalised at seven, when her wheelchair was taken from her, and she was put in a 'cot' and left to some unfathomable existence. Jane is very clear that she had a deep

DOI: 10.4324/9781351169929-8

desire to prove those responsible for her ending up in this predicament, completely wrong.

The child, by default, now has two, perhaps three, foci – learning to walk and looking to please, and possibly to prove. Immediate improvement in performance may be held in abeyance whilst the child orientates around what is expected of them: 'don't cry, try again, stand up, smile, it's alright'. The interruptions are endless and may intrude on the child's flow in ways the observer cannot construe.

And there is a caution here, as James Hillman (2017) writes in *The Soul's Code*, 'They (children) are trying to live two lives at once, the one they were born with, and the one, of the place and among the people they were born into'. Almost immediately a child is being asked to adopt cultural norms to win 'approval' and to prove they are worthy. So perhaps Steve Borthwick was right when he added 'prove' in our conversation.

Many of us, including almost all the people interviewed for this book, have had the experience, generally as a child, of moments when we flowed on a river of time, aligned and in flow within our ecosystem. Time slowed down; we were living life. All seemed to be magical, as if life was living us. On some days, perhaps we got together with friends, got out in the streets or fields, and made magic and mischief. It was being called to the adventure and exploration of life, the unfolding moments that didn't require anything of us other than curiosity and to engage with life, so that we might live it fully, that was the goal, and pretty much as Joseph Campbell outlines it in *The Hero with a Thousand Faces*, answering the call to adventure is just the beginning.

Further, in the International Journal of Golf Science, I came across this paragraph,

> The dimensions measured by this instrument (of flow) are challenge-skill balance, action-awareness merging, clear goals, unambiguous feedback, concentration on task at hand, sense of control, loss of self-consciousness, transformation of time, and autotelic experience. Jackson and Eklund (2012, p. 350) state together the nine dimensions 'represent the optimal psychological state of flow; by themselves, they signify conceptual elements of the flow experience.'
>
> (Pates et al., 2012)

It's as if the authors are describing my way of being as a child, as I was growing into myself, it was being, not task that gave me the optimal psychological fulfilment and performance on a daily basis, especially during the summer break.

If there was a task, it was satisfying our curiosity at what about the world. I did this in the East End of London in the 1960s, with kids of all races, creed, and colour, amongst still bombed out houses from World War II and in the many parks and on the canals; flow knows no boundaries, it discriminates against no one.

Lynn Barnett (1976) in her paper, 'Play and Intrinsic Rewards: A Reply to Csikszentmihalyi' writes, 'Any naïve observer of children's play, or that of adults for that matter, could describe the long and continuous durations of activity sometimes with only one object'. Barnett writes this in reply to Csikszentmihalyi's assertion that 'flow is difficult to maintain for any length of time without at least momentary interruptions', and this plays to the earlier point, we are constantly and consistently interrupted, and it becomes a norm and until, one could venture, the advent of the smart phone, we had pretty much learned to cope. And it is also contradicted by the endless hours spent being with friends as a child that were only interrupted by the summoning from someone that the sun was going down and that supper was on the table.

Born to Flow asserts that flow is present and completely immersive in those early years, when we were unencumbered by the 'forgetting' that was about to descend through our participation in 'growing up', where the increase in interruptions is so obviously exponential, and where constant communication and social media, stream at us 24 hours a day, 7 days a week, 365 days a year, every year. A total of 86,400 seconds a day are open to interruption and distraction if you do not control your mindset and attention.

It is clear that flow is present through play, facilitating that unbelievably creative activity when the fertile, febrile imagination is cutting loose. We can see this with adults using LSP (Lego© Serious Play™), for example, to solve deeply complex issues, problems, or opportunities that teams or organisations face. They forget that they are at 'work' and begin to explore through the medium of a child's toy, perhaps reconnecting with something deeply innate, rekindling their flow through curiosity. For adults, it is perhaps a re-enchantment with everyday life, as it were.

And society encouraged us to play in those early years, nodding approvingly until it decided that play was no longer on the curriculum. Society confused, and still does, 'childlike' with 'childish' and therefore with something unworthy of attention and we move from the unfettered to the compliant. I have seen this on occasions when, as a certified LSP™ facilitator, pitching it as an option for problem solving, there can be a default to 'but this is a child's toy'. But once participants are involved and engaged in flow, magic happens and 'serious' problems are solved, issues resolved, and opportunities explored.

In one particular intervention over three days, a limited company, through serious play and spending time in the ocean learning to surf (another flow enhancer), found that it was the 'wrong shape, facing the wrong way' and as such, at the end of the workshop changed its legal status; such is the power of play in flow. And in yet another intervention using LSP™, a participant who had been particularly scathing about the fact we would facilitate a learning and development day using 'a toy', was, at the end of the day completely immersed, on a table, in the middle of an LSP model, adding their own, authentic flow voice.

As Barnett (1976) writes in her paper,

> The alternative that I would like to present is that structured settings be modified to allow the individual the opportunity to interact in whatever manner is intrinsically rewarding to himself (sic). Rather than to structure activities within the setting to conform to what one individual, feels would be enjoyable to others.

And in my master's thesis 'Exploring the Perceptions of Purchasers of Coaching Services towards Coaching in the Natural Environment', subtitled, 'Why Don't They Get out of the Box?' i.e., the 12 × 12 meeting room, I explored why organisations felt and needed at the time to have coaching conform to that meeting room setting when, as has been subsequently adopted and much more common today, it is seen as beneficial 'in context' to get the coachee out of the environment that may constrict thinking into one that can enhance their flow. In the same thesis I asserted that 'the barriers to breakthrough in performance are often embedded in the environment where we need to perform the most'; by definition, where we should be enabled to do our best work, fully flowing.

As children, when we started to 'transition' through early years, we were no longer masters of our own flow; we were usurped by societal demands to conform. It is a sad moment when we move from experimenting and learning through play to the constraining and confining curriculum of 'learning to work', as if that is not what play is. Play accommodates all of our imagination, and curiosity, our intellect, and our emotions; play is where we reach, unfettered, for the stars. And as we will discover, curiosity and engagement, key to play, are key to this journey too. Noel Coward famously said, 'work is much more fun than fun', and perhaps he was right if we develop a culture and ecosystem that enable us to develop our predisposition for flow.

Almost by necessity, the analogy of flowing water permeates this book and for good reason, the way that the water carves its way through the world is an expression of its flow through it, through energy draining igneous rock or slicing and carving effortlessly through the sedimentary. *Born to Flow* argues that the activities of everyday life could be considered an expression of your flow through life, just like a child learning to stand and walk, or a river beginning to flow.

What is interesting about the child's adventure is that they have no idea that they are in flow, more than that, they have no idea of flow. They are simply being, fulfilling an evolutionary request to flow forwards. And as the late Irish poet, John O'Donoghue wrote in an unfinished poem, 'I wish I could live like a river flows, carried by the surprise of its own unfolding', which of course would mean remembering he was born to flow.

As mentioned, received wisdom has it that 'flow', is a 'state' that you 'get into', and not something that is demonstrably present – but if we witness the child at play, flow is ably demonstrated through being. This simple misunderstanding, that flow is a state to get into, can have the effect that we spend most of our lives with distraction and disruption disabling our innate flow, running from one task to the next in search of something elusive; there is a Polynesian proverb, 'standing on the back of a whale, fishing for minnows'. So, it might be with flow, it's closer than we think.

As George Kelly (2003) writes at the very beginning of his seminal work, *The Psychology of Personal Constructs*, 'that each man (sic) contemplates in his own personal way the stream of events on which he finds himself swiftly borne'.

We can see the child, in flow, gets to a point where crawling along, literally or metaphorically, is no longer sufficient and, in flow, experiments, observes, and tries things out, eventually, literally, finding its feet, as a pedestrian, a runner, perhaps a dancer, an athlete, or in Jane's case, a person confined to a wheelchair, who both scubas and skis; the wheelchair has not impeded her desire to flow.

Paradoxically something has happened during our evolution that has enabled us to perhaps flow at a faster rate than other species. We have cast off the shackles of inefficient movement and realised our ability to stand above it all to have the advantage of being a biped.

However, it seems, as a species we have amnesia, we have forgotten that we are born to flow and if we could re-connect with the innate potential that flow enables us to express, we would find a re-enchantment with ourselves and with our environment that has been submerged in the detritus of simply trying to survive the many kinds of friction that intrude, outside of our intrusive thoughts.

In essence, these pages are not only about flow, but they are also about construing, memory, and remembering of actively calling to mind, from days that may seem far away and distant, a joy and a connection with the world, which is childlike in its innocence but not childish in its intent. And John O'Donohue (2009) talks about the latent potentiality in us in his wonderful book, *Anam Cara*, which translates as 'soul friend', the person to whom you could reveal the depths of your soul, "When you cease to fear your solitude, a new creativity awakens within you. Your forgotten wealth begins to reveal itself'.

As stated earlier, remembering is an excellent way to reconnect back into your ever-present flow in a meaningful and significant way. Kelly (2003) said,

Nor has the stream of the individual man's (sic) life escaped the attention of curious students. The highly articulate William James was fascinated by the currents and eddies in the stream of consciousness. The inarticulate Adolph Meyer urged his students to draw a timeline through the facts of their patients' lives. The sensitive Sigmund Freud waded into the headwaters of the stream in a search for the underground springs which fed it. And the impulsive Henri Bergson jumped from the bank into the current and, as he was carried along, speculated that mind could be used as a yardstick for measuring time. As for personal ways of looking at things: Solomon, in writing about the worried man, said, "as he thinketh in his heart, so he is.

So, we can see, as stated earlier, that the word 'flow' has currency, and in terms of constructive alternativism, Kelly connected with the flow of water, and indeed consciousness, to help readers reflect on how great thinkers helped him carve his way through the bedrock of psychology, like a river through a metaphorical canyon. And the nod to the stoic, and indeed mindset, with the Solomon quote, which in itself is interesting for the phraseology, 'as he thinketh in his heart' (also to be found in Proverbs 23:7 KJV) which ties the emotions firmly to the stoic.

All that is required at this stage is that you observe a baby learning to walk or a child or, come to that, an adult at play, and that you cast your mind back and you remember your flow moments because therein lies the payoff of recognising that flow is always present. And as Jim Rohn famously said, 'Success leaves clues'.

As Lyall Watson (1973, p. 23) writes in 'Supernature', 'Grey Walter, the discoverer of several basic rhythmic patterns of the brain, puts it perfectly: He says that the most significant thing about a pattern is that you can remember it and compare it with another pattern'.

Therefore, if you can remember an experience or a pattern in, or of, your flow from childhood or early adulthood, you may be able to recognise, compare, and replicate that pattern at will. You start to own your flow experience through remembering that it was there at the very beginning, and having that awareness or recollection is a key.

If an idea from Gestalt therapy, that awareness is curative, is correct, and it is possible to envisage an existence whereby we are in flow all the time, developing heightened awareness allows us to access what I think is barely hidden beneath the surface. The distraction and disruption from flow is what makes it harder to recognise and remember.

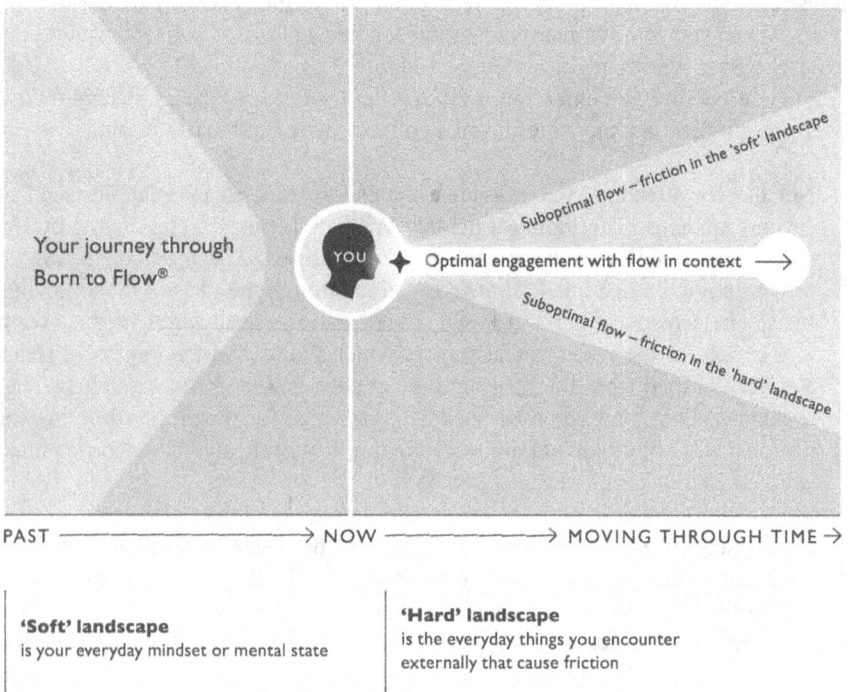

PAST ————————→ NOW ——————→ MOVING THROUGH TIME →

'Soft' landscape
is your everyday mindset or mental state

'Hard' landscape
is the everyday things you encounter externally that cause friction

Born to Flow®

Figure 7.1 The landscape of Born to Flow.

Immersed in everyday life, we capitulate to the baser instinct of trying to survive and the fact that living in flow might be more efficient, creative, or productive, is lost to us. The truth is that flow requires expression, and we must undam it. In essence, I think we are coming from flow into our future or activity, not using the activity or task to produce flow. Think about that for a minute and the flow notion is turned on its head, and why not challenge the notion? Liberation from the tyranny of 'trying to get into flow' is a step towards increased performance. As Yoda says in Star Wars, 'Do or do not, there is no "try"' (Kasdan & Brackett, 1978). The flow is there, accept it as a fundamental and innate way of being, free up the energy wasted on trying.

The picture that should be emerging, is an upended view of what it is to flow. As stated earlier, the original 'flow' diagram perpetuated the myth that up is always the best direction of travel; the flow channel goes up, from bottom left to top right. But I reiterate here, going forwards is probably more symptomatic of what most of us are trying to do in life – flow forwards – like a river returning to the source.

Born to Flow's basic representation of the flow channel (Figure 7.1), critically puts you in the frame and by the end of the book, it will be populated with the constituent parts that we meet in the journey of life. At the conclusion, you will also find a template to populate with your own causes of friction or flow inhibitors. But for now, I think forward is a great place to start.

Summary

In this chapter, we see and consider:

- One of the most wonderful things that we can witness is a baby or small child, totally engaged in learning through play and flow is present through play. And as Lynn Barnett said, 'any naïve observer of children's play, or that of adults for that matter, could describe the long and continuous durations of activity sometimes with only one object'.
- When we witness the child at play, flow is ably demonstrated through being and our potential, that flow enables us to express, emerges as performance because play accommodates all of our imagination, curiosity, intellect, emotions; play is where we reach, unfettered, for the stars.
- One element of what we are seeing in moments such as these is a being 'in flow' and as George Kelly says, a being in motion, not a body, and yet at child's first stumble when someone intervenes, then they could disrupt the child's flow permanently; they could slip from being completely flowing to where there's an overwhelming impulse to please and to prove because of the feedback the child is receiving. A young child, by default, has two, or perhaps three, foci – learning to walk and looking to please, and to prove. 'Performance' may be held in abeyance whilst a child orientates around feedback they're given.

- As per James Hillman, 'They (children) are trying to live two lives at once, the one they were born with, and the one of the place and among the people they were born into'.
- A child is expected to adopt cultural norms very early on in their life to win 'approval'; to prove they are worthy, but flow is present and completely immersive in early years, when we are unencumbered by the 'forgetting' that descends through our involvement in 'growing up'.
- Society confused, and still does, 'childlike' with 'childish'.
- 'The barriers to breakthrough in performance are often embedded in the environment where we need to perform the most', Cliff Kimber unpublished MSc. Thesis.
- 'I wish I could live like a river flows, carried by the surprise of its own unfolding', said John O'Donoghue.

Exercise/Reflective Practice

1   Consider if, on waking, you feel any flow. Perhaps the remnants of a flow dream or perhaps how sleep has enabled recovery from a day at the gym. Decide how and what you are measuring when feeling and thinking about the flow you wake to. Use something to record your thoughts and feelings.

Interview Insights and Deep Thoughts with Charles Hazelwood, Conductor, on His Experience of Flow

- 'You can lead a horse to water, but you can't make it drink, so it's (humans/flow) got to have hunger for it itself'.
- 'What we've learned now is something much, much better, much healthier, much more holistic, and much more successful, which is, the best way to get the best out of a team of people, is to create a really strong, secure environment within which they can shine brighter than they ever thought possible'.
- (Flow) 'it's all about my body and how I use my body. It's quite strange. It's like alchemy. You know, when it's working, there is an extraordinary flow'.
- (In terms of flow) 'I have every reason to support and nourish and believe in my authenticity'.
- 'Every human being has an authentic response to something which is valuable'.
- 'Babies are authentic, right, they are absolutely authentic, they cry, they shout, they laugh, they dance, they fart, that they are just authentically themselves. And then bit by bit, they start to learn how to be culturally normal, So, they start to kind of, put away their instinctive responses to things, they start to try to learn to be a bit more like other people are, to wear the clothes other people wear, to use the terms of phrase other people use. So, bit by bit, they lose their authenticity, and one of the biggest problems in our culture is that it takes so long to find it again'.

- 'The voice in my head was saying if you can find your authentic self, rather, if you can trust it, and endorse it and embrace it, then you are actually free to do all the things that you'd really like to do'.
- 'So, I found all that flow. And then only to have it. kind of, completely drummed out of me with my first bloody and bruising encounters with the professional business'.
- (Flow) 'Well, this is a long slow process learning to trust myself. Yes, learn to believe in my own innate and useful and valuable proficiencies. We so often slightly cauterize our sixth senses at work'.
- 'Someone without flow I feel great pity for, who wants to be stuck? Or blocked? We all know what it feels like when you do something, and it really flows, like you make a great meal. And the kind of the pushback you get from that is insane'.
- (In flow) 'Everything elegantly connects up'.
- 'My version of that (old saying) is lying on your death bed wishing that you just allowed yourself more flow'.
- 'If the boss had any sense, they'd create an environment where their team will be coming up with really shit hot ideas, which then by the way, would make the boss look really cool, too'.
- (In the future) 'I would always want to pay more attention to my flow. I think it would be about being more in touch with myself, every moment of the day and to be clearer about my feelings, clear with people'.
- 'I think it's combination of the two actually, (preternatural and natural) it's a natural state that says that all babies are born with flow'.
- 'This universe has flow when love is its dominant theme'.

References

Barnett, L. (1976). Play and Intrinsic Rewards: a Reply To Csikszentmihalyi. *Journal of Humanistic Psychology, 16*(3), 83–87. https://doi.org/10.1177/002216787601600312 (Original work published 1976)

Brown, D. E. (2004). Human universals, human nature & human culture. *Daedalus, 133*(4), 47–54.

Campbell, J. (1993). *The hero with a thousand faces.* Fontana Press.

Hillman, J. (2017). *The soul's code: In search of character and calling.* Ballantine Books.

Kasdan, L., & Brackett, L. (1978). The empire strikes back. Screenplay.

Kelly, G. (2003). *The psychology of personal constructs: Volume one.* Routledge.

O'Donohue, J. (2009). *Anam cara: A book of Celtic wisdom.* Harper Collins.

Pates, J., Cowen, A. P., & Karageorghis, C. I. (2012). The effect of a client-centered approach on flow states and the performance of three elite golfers. *International Journal of Golf Science, 1*(2), 113–126.

Watson, L. (1973). *Supernature: The history of the supernatural.* Coronet/Hodder London.

Chapter 8

Where the Flow Begins

Estuarine

If there is a prenatal flow, then it is concerned with autonomic processes firstly and then, when the foetus has developed in the third trimester, Christof Koch, writing in Scientific American, says, 'Exposure to maternal speech sounds in the muffled confines of the womb enables the foetus to pick up statistical regularities so that the new-born can distinguish its mother's voice and even her language from others'[1] and perhaps in those muffled confines, we find the headwaters, the first trickle of flow bubbling up.

Is the act of gaining awareness so closely linked to flow that we hardly notice it and put all of our attention into being absorbed by the world? For that is what the world will surely do, absorb us if we let it, until our own uniqueness simply disappears into obscurity. Absorbed into a world from the very first independent gasp, as the umbilical cord is severed, and in turn we are severed from the unique embryonic environment where we have been steadily growing and knitting the delicate matter of consciousness.

We then continue the journey through life with all the advantages of a species that has been assiduously adaptive in ways that other species have not over the past millennia, we have, and perhaps continue to, emerged from an evolutionary odyssey that is born out of an inquisitive and curious lump of grey jelly carried around on a bipedal frame that enables us to flow, the constituents of which may be much older than we realise.

If flow is to be defined by a commonality, then the current received wisdom from the original research of a person in relation to a task has ticked all the boxes, as we saw earlier. But we must take into account that the received construct of 'flow' is predicated on the researcher's interpretation of someone else's construct of 'flow'. Thus, we slip ever further into researching where the light is and not where the light could be. To illuminate; a person is walking down a pitch-black road when in the distance they see a streetlamp and under the streetlamp someone on hands and knees. As they get closer, they see a person is searching for something on the ground, directly under the light. 'Hey, what's up?'. The person looks up, 'I've lost my car keys'. Our friendly traveller drops to the ground to help with the search and after 15 minutes or so turns to the other

DOI: 10.4324/9781351169929-9

and says, 'There are no keys here', to which comes the reply, 'No, but there is a light'! The basis for this anecdote is attributed to Nasreddin and is an often-told tale from Sufi culture.

Prenatal existence seems to be nothing but two alternate states of sleep, according to Koch (2009), 'the foetus is suspended in a warm and dark cave, connected to the placenta that pumps blood, nutrients and hormones into its growing body and brain, the foetus is asleep'.

Invasive experiments in rat and lamb pups and observational studies using ultrasound and electrical recordings in humans show that the third-trimester foetus is almost always in one of these two sleep states. Called active and quiet sleep, these states can be distinguished using electroencephalography (EEG). Their different EEG signatures go hand in hand with distinct behaviours: Breathing, swallowing, licking, and moving the eyes, but no large-scale body movements in active sleep; no breathing, no eye movements and tonic muscle activity in quiet sleep. These stages correspond to rapid-eye-movement (REM) and slow-wave sleep common to all mammals. In late gestation, the foetus is in one of these two sleep states 95% of the time, separated by brief transitions. What is fascinating is the discovery that the foetus is actively sedated by the low oxygen pressure (equivalent to that at the top of Mount Everest), the warm and cushioned uterine environment, and a range of neuroinhibitory and sleep-inducing substances produced by the placenta and the foetus itself: adenosine; two steroidal anaesthetics, allopregnanolone and pregnanolone; one potent hormone, prostaglandin D_2; and others.

So, not much flow going on there unless one considers 'flow' as a way of being, biologically, rather than a task of doing. Existence in 'the cave' is simply getting 'ready' for the journey, 'slow flow', perhaps.

What the foetus is about to endure as it emerges into the world, almost fully formed, but ill equipped, is so profoundly different that this might be the first real interruption to a pure form of flow. However, as Joseph Campbell says in the first episode of 'The Power of Myth' with Bill Moyes,

> Otto Rank, in his wonderful, very short book called The Myth of the Birth of the Hero, says that everyone is a hero in his birth. He has undergone a tremendous transformation from a little, you might say, water creature. Living in a realm of the amniotic fluid and so forth, then coming out, becoming an air-breathing mammal that ultimately will be self-standing and so forth, is an enormous transformation and it is a heroic act, and it's a heroic act on the mother's part to bring it about. It's the primary hero, hero form, you might say.

So perhaps if we are heroic at the beginning of this journey, we call life, then perhaps we are also born to flow, and to our detriment we forget both as we grow older.

In *Democracy in America* by Alexis de Tocqueville (2015), published in 1835, we can see that this way of thinking about a child's arrival and the impact of the world on them has occupied others for some time. He writes,

> After the birth of a human being his early years are obscurely spent in the toils or pleasures of childhood. As he grows up the world receives him, when his manhood begins, and he enters into contact with his fellows. He is then studied for the first time, and it is imagined that the germ of the vices and the virtues of his mature years is then formed. This, if I am not mistaken, is a great error. We must begin higher up; we must watch the infant in its mother's arms; we must see the first images which the external world casts upon the dark mirror of his mind; the first occurrences which he witnesses; we must hear the first words which awaken the sleeping powers of thought, and stand by his earliest efforts, if we would understand the prejudices, the habits, and the passions which will rule his life. The entire man is, so to speak, to be seen in the cradle of the child.

And we can see the power of enabling children and to a greater or lesser extent getting out of their way, in the words of Gibran and Bushrui (2012, p. 81) in *The Prophet* when they write,

> You may give them (children) your love but not your thoughts, for they have their own thoughts. You may house their bodies but not their souls, for their soul's dwell in the house of tomorrow, which you cannot visit, even in your dreams. You may strive to be like them, but seek not to make them like you, for life goes not backward, nor tarries with yesterday. You are the bows from which your children as living arrows are sent forth.

If consciousness is a prerequisite for flow, then awareness must follow closely and perhaps, as research shows, because infants have very scant regard for themselves until about 18 months, the immersion and absorption in the new environment is not overly surprising. Self-awareness in relation to our awareness of 'other' and generally awareness of ourselves as beings in motion in an ever-changing environment enable us to start to navigate with childlike wonder and curiosity. And curiosity may be the spark that lights the way in all our endeavours.

At this early stage, experimentation is the continuous feedback loop, and we should remember that everything, and anything we do for the first time is an experiment; we are on the journey of sense making in this brand-new world and unencumbered by the societal pressures and community tribalism that will soon envelop us. For the moment we are enjoying the neural plasticity and the muscular tensions that start to enable movement. Some will crawl and some will scoot along on their bottom, but for most the journey is to move and to start to reach upwards, but also forwards, into the future that is coming towards us and that we will have the chance to shape if we participate. It's also of interest to remember that our presence in the world changes the world, even if we ourselves are not cognisant of it.

What else then would indicate that we are born to flow? It would seem in the early stages of life, that as a species, we are drawn to utilise all the potential we have, and the body seems to have developed a reward system for our efforts. Hans Henrick Knoop (2002) talks well to this point in *Play, Learning and Creativity: Why Happy Children Are Better Learners*,

> one of the most important driving forces in the development of both children and adults is the positive feelings with which the body rewards us when we learn something important. The body uses positive feelings to help encourage us to learn what is important for us, since effective learning has been aiding us in our struggle to survive ever since the stone ages. One of the most important of these feelings is sometimes referred to as Flow.

Perhaps the way we 'feel' in relation to our flow is a good measure of our flow at any one time, if we are looking for a measure. Feeling rather than thinking perhaps, because as Laird Hamilton, legendary big wave surfer, innovator (co-inventor of tow-in surfing), and entrepreneur, said during our conversation, 'I think that when things are optimal, thinking is probably too slow'.

I think this plays to what Vivak Ranadivé and Kevin Maney (2011, p. 48) were alluding to in *The Two Second Advantage*

> Flow seems to be a state of pure predictiveness. The person in a state of flow is firing complex chunks so rapidly and seamlessly that she feels like she can see what's going to happen before it happens and can act with complete certainty and confidence. It's easier to be confident when you know how things will turn out.

Notwithstanding that they refer to the 'flow state' it adds an interesting dynamic to the complex process of flow and what might be achieved through its practice; you're probably not going to be able to predict the future but maybe you will start to identify more options as you continue to build your flow skillset.

And Justin Hughes, builds on this idea when he says this of graduating from a first year Red Arrows pilot to a third-year pilot, 'You get to the point where in your pattern recognition, you don't recognise the pattern, you recognise anomalies in the pattern, because you've seen the pattern so many times'. Justin's point is useful if we are trying to recall flow moments that were significant in our growth, and we can anchor back to them using our latent potentiality for flow.

Ranadivé and Maney (2011, p. 48) also talk about Gary Klein, formerly associated with Applied Research Associates, and probably best known for his book *Seeing What Others Don't: The Remarkable Ways We Gain Insights*, and his work on anticipatory thinking, not only in individuals but in teams. In an unpublished work with co-authors, David Snowden and Chew Lock Pin, and given in manuscript form to Maney, Klein asserts 'we believe that anticipatory thinking is critical to effective performance for individuals and teams'. Klein also postulates that the better we get at something, the more we can predict what might not happen.

For Laird Hamilton, his rescue teams are looking for what happens when Laird wipes out on a colossal wave, predicting where he is going to surface and being there as fast as possible, it's life or death. It's the kind of faculty that Wayne Gretzky used to predict where the puck was going to be, famously stating, 'A good hockey player plays where the puck is. A great hockey player plays where the puck is going to be' in the book *Playing with Fire* by Theo Fleury, Kirstie McLellen Day, and Wayne Gretzky (2009).

It would appear that defining flow starts with basic human states and traits related to being i.e., consciousness, awareness, self-awareness, self-management, curiosity, movement, interpersonal skills, and a desire to fulfil our potential, which is fuelled by an intrinsic reward system that has developed to keep us learning important lessons, but as interestingly, might also have developed to enable flow as a way of being.

Only as we have, allegedly, become more intelligent and sophisticated have we let our flow dilute through our immersion and absorption in roles and responsibilities, tasks, and identities, till we barely have cognisance of it, or remember we have it, and by definition access to it, convincing ourselves that focus on tasks or goals is the answer to all issues, problems, and opportunities.

As Hippocrates (460–370BCE) wrote in *The Sacred Disease*,

> Men ought to know that from the human brain and from the brain only arise our pleasures, joys, laughter, and jests as well as our sorrows, pains, griefs and tears ……it is the same thing which makes us mad or delirious, inspires us with dread and fear, whether by night or day, brings us sleeplessness, inopportune mistakes, aimless anxieties, absent-mindedness and acts that are contrary to habit.

Known as the father of medicine, Hippocrates has perhaps placed the brain and mind as the home of construing flow because if, as he points out, the mind and brain are responsible for all the above, then perhaps flow has its root there too, if not within our biology.

If flow is a construct of mind that manifests itself through our expression and our purposefulness then, who but us, can own that construct, it makes little sense that someone else should dictate the nature of our experience or our reality or our flowfulness.

It is worth remembering that to re-route a river comes at a cost and often, unforeseen consequences, as Knutson Morrison found out when building a dam in Afghanistan, thereby causing the water table to push salt to the surface, ideal conditions for poppies to grow in abundance, and as an unforeseen consequence, according to Adam Curtis in his insightful documentary, 'Hyper-normalisation', Afghanistan is now one of the world's largest producers of opium.

To fully express ourselves through flow, we must untangle it from task. Task doesn't explain why you are doing or what you are doing, it merely requires you to do it. As a person expressing myself, I might choose to tackle a task in a specific way and find huge enjoyment in it. I might also understand that if it is challenging, I need to up-skill; if it is boring, I can challenge my curiosity to find something interesting in it for me in relation to the task, but it is 'I', as a being in motion, who is expressing my flow intent, not the tasks requirement for me to be in flow to tackle it or perform at an elite level. This is an important distinction; flow is expressing through me as a being in motion. And if flow is a state, then perhaps it is the 'I' who leaves 'it'.

Another question poses itself almost effortlessly and along with other general adaptive responses: Flow may be an older human trait that sits alongside 'fight or flight'. The question to consider is perhaps this: If fight or flight is an evolutionary response to surviving, should we consider flow in much the same way, as if we are born with fight and flight etched in our being, perhaps the ability to flow also exists there? Like fight or flight, flow is an inherent part of our make-up.

One could argue that our senses, in parts of the world and for many different reasons, have been made dull, are less attuned, less prepared for the fight or flight, than they were perhaps a hundred or a thousand years ago, or argue that society has changed; it has led us to dial down these responses somewhat, thus we are less prepared when something goes awry. In the same way that humans have sought to exert control over their habitat, the oldest man-made structure is a windbreak, some 1.8 million years old in Olduvai Gorge in Tanzania, by regulating temperature, we have wandered, paradoxically, into an environment of our own making, where the keenness of our senses have been dulled by our desire to create a stable environment, which is paradoxical in a VUCA (volatility, uncertainty, complexity, ambiguity) world. Fight and flight are survival responses from threats to our safety, and this instinct is common in many creatures, not just the hominidae.

If the sympathetic and parasympathetic nervous systems have evolved in such a way to protect us from harm, what is there to say that the innate flow ability is not inherent and perhaps evolved from the time when humans experienced their environment differently. Perhaps absorbed in being, might we consider that other evolutionary traits have survived to enable us at other higher levels of being, rather than the baser instincts of 'fight' or 'flight'.

Perhaps it is this early state, that man, as Daisetz Zuzuki states in his introduction to *Zen in the Art of Archery* by Eugen Herrigel, when writing about the art of self-forgetfulness,

> Man thinks yet he does not think. He thinks like the showers coming down from the sky; he thinks like waves rolling on the ocean; he thinks like the stars illuminating the nightly heavens; he thinks like the green foliage shooting forth in the relaxing spring breeze. Indeed, he is the showers, the ocean, the stars, the foliage.

This idea may not be as fanciful as it first seems given the role that specialised chemicals released during the fight or flight response also play a key role in the way that humans can increase their flow, for example, norepinephrine, a precursor to dopamine, plays a key role in all three 'Fs': Fight, flight, and flow. Perhaps flow is biology at play. And to add to the earlier point about other non-human species experiencing fright or flight responses, a paper published in 2023 by Sara Hintz and Jason Lee is reversing our myopic view of what flow is and thinking about flow in animals and how we might study their experience of flow in their world[7].

Obliquely, if flight and fight are regarded as first stages of 'general adaptation response' i.e., kill or be killed, one observes that this response incorporates key elements of what might be regarded as the flow canon, for example, challenge, clarity of task, clear goal, overcoming a physical or psychological barrier; in other words, conquering a task through increasing flow.

Summary

In this chapter, we see and explore:

- 'Exposure to maternal speech sounds in the womb enables the foetus to pick up statistical regularities so that the newborn can distinguish its mother's voice'. Christof Koch states, 'Prenatal existence seems to be nothing but two alternate states of sleep, the foetus is suspended in a warm and dark cave, connected to the placenta that pumps blood, nutrients and hormones into its growing body and brain, the foetus is asleep' and as the umbilical cord is severed, and in turn we are severed from the unique embryonic environment where we have been steadily growing and knitting the delicate matter of consciousness.
- We start the journey through life with all the advantages of a species that has been assiduously adaptive in ways that other species have not, carried around on a bipedal frame that enables us to flow.
- Self-awareness in relation to our awareness of 'other' and awareness of ourselves as beings in motion enable us to start to navigate with childlike wonder and curiosity. Curiosity may be the spark that lights the way in all our endeavours.
- 'The body uses positive feelings to help encourage us to learn what is important for us, since effective learning has been aiding us in our struggle to survive since the stone age. One of the most important of these feelings is sometimes referred to as Flow'.
- It would appear that defining flow starts with basic human states and traits related to being i.e., consciousness, awareness, self-awareness, curiosity, movement, and a desire to fulfil our potential, which is fuelled by an intrinsic reward system.
- If flow is a construct of the mind that manifests itself through our expression and our purposefulness, then, who but us, can own that construct.
- Task doesn't explain why you are doing or what you are doing, it merely requires you to do it, and flow is expressing through a being in motion.

- Obliquely, if flight and fight are regarded as first stages of 'general adaptation response' i.e., kill or be killed, one observes that this response incorporates key elements of what might be regarded as the 'flow orthodoxy', for example, challenge, clarity of task, clear goal, overcoming a physical or psychological barrier; in other words, conquering a task through increasing flow.

Exercise/Reflective Practice

1 Consider what else in your life you accept because it is axiomatic i.e., something that is self-evidently true, that few people would argue against because it has some kind of intrinsic merit, and it cannot be proved or disproved. Make a list, for example, the whole is greater than the part.
2 What do you do because you have an innate feeling that you must do it: Poetry, calculus, drawing, etc. Can you articulate in very clear terms *what* is trying to express through these activities?
3 When you engage in something you enjoy because it is either a calling or you have been curious enough to discover it, do you find it easier to let go of distractions?
4 How might you develop letting go of distractions as a practice to recognise and increase your flow?

References

de Tocqueville, A. (2015). *Democracy in America: Vol. I and II*. Read Books Ltd.

Fleury, T., Day, K. M., & Gretzky, W. (2009). *Playing with fire*. Triumph Books.

Gibran, K., & Bushrui, S. B. (2012). *The prophet: A new annotated edition*. Simon and Schuster.

Hintze, S., & Yee, J. R. (2023). Animals in flow – towards the scientific study of intrinsic reward in animals. *Biological Reviews of the Cambridge Philosophical Society*, 98(3), 792–806. https://doi.org/10.1111/brv.12930.

Knoop, H. H. (2002). *Play, learning and creativity-why happy children are better learners*. Aschehoug.

Koch, C. (2009). When does consciousness arise. *Scientific American Mind*, 20(5), 20–21.

Ranadivé, V., & Maney, K. (2011). *The two-second advantage: How we succeed by anticipating the future–just enough*. Crown Publishing Group.

Chapter 9

Flow Science?

Tributary

'Flow was a black box, an astoundingly intriguing phenomenon accessible only through subjective recall', says Steven Kotler in an article for Time magazine and further adds,

> the neurochemistry of flow. A team of neuroscientists at Bonn University in Germany discovered that endorphins are definitely part of flow's cocktail and, as other researchers have determined, so are norepinephrine, dopamine, anandamide, and serotonin. All five (sic) are pleasure-inducing, performance-enhancing neurochemicals, upping everything from muscle reaction times to attention, pattern recognition and lateral thinking—the three horsemen of rapid-fire problem-solving.

In thinking about being born to flow over the last 20 years or so, mainly in relation to sport, but also in trying to understand why I felt the way I did, as I flowed through my life, I struggled to understand where flow was if it wasn't there all the time. I wondered if it was a mindset, or mental state, of if it was a by-product of those chemicals inducing a kind of hypnotic state. But flow is more than a chemically induced by-product of response to the release of these pleasure-inducing chemicals. What comes first – flow to release the chemicals or the chemicals to induce flow?

It appeared, from my construing, that the people around me were moving and therefore, at some level, they were flowing. They were 'beings in motion'. It also struck me that people seemed to move up and down a flow scale in some way. And I wondered if it was some kind of vicarious or collaborative flow. When people are 'flowing' especially in a team, does it make it easier for those around them to flow?

I would watch my Dad, a master upholsterer at work, and he would be in full flow. Back in the day, he would take a handful of tacks (a small, broad headed nail), put them in his mouth and with a magnetic hammer, he would extract them one at a time from between his teeth on the magnetic end of the hammer and as he was holding the stretched fabric in place on the frame of the armchair, he would spin the hammer as he aimed so the tack was facing the fabric and he would land it in exactly the right place. I was awe struck and not even tempted to try it. But I

DOI: 10.4324/9781351169929-10

noticed I was in flow watching the man in flow, and as I think back, I know it was some kind of vicarious or collaborative flow.

But I also noticed when his flow was diminished, I say diminished because I always saw a 'light on' somewhere within him, I always noticed his flow scaling up or down, in his battle with seasonal affective disorder (SAD), haunted by migraine and later in life, cardio-vascular disease, but his flow was there, in being entranced when catching dawns light whilst course fishing, in just walking the dog through the forest, and in being with my mum – always flow. And when I watched him literally take his last breath, flow was completely, utterly, irreducibly gone. No flow.

When I spoke with Jonny Wilkinson, former England international rugby player and now host of the very successful podcast 'I AM' with his brother Mark 'sparks' Wilkinson in July 2024, he mentioned the idea that when he was working with someone as their kicking coach, his flow might impact the players' flow, could it be, if he knew he was in flow, that he could enable more flow in the kicker? We kicked the thought around and settled on the idea that it was entirely possible that this kind of transference could happen.

The first Kotler quote above is from a 2008 article by founder of the Flow Genome project, Steven Kotler; the key word in that sentence is 'subjective'. It is a critical piece of information on your journey towards increasing your flow, simply because it indicates what I have been saying, that if you can remember (recall) and if you can recognise times when you have been in 'flow', then you are construing your own flow reality. And, as you build on that subjective recall or remembering, you will notice that it gets easier to recognise flow in yourself and in others. You notice where flow is absent, in the dead or in the inanimate, as where there is flow, there is life.

It is one of nature's purest axioms. Unless you accept Professor Leroy Little Bear's assertion that, 'in Aboriginal philosophy, existence consists of energy. All things are animate, imbued with spirit'.

The word 'flow' has been appropriated to mean only one thing, peak or optimal performance, as we saw earlier, and according to Susan Jackson 1999 (revised 2000), this is more, 'a standard of accomplishment' whereas flow, is described as, 'optimal psychological state'. Perhaps construing flow in only these terms may be debilitating in the extreme for all of those in sport or business, further, in life in general, who are striving to meet their better selves. Why is it either/or, not and/both? And if it is and/both, do we consider broadening the definition of flow?

Currently the canonical belief dictates that only when a set of criteria, mainly outside of one's own control, falls into place, when the perfect storm is upon us, then we transcend our existence and ascend to some special state where we linger for a short period of time before thumping back into the 'norm', where we are allowed to marvel at the change in our state, where during our task or activity, we were 'outside' of ourselves, in that special zone, just left of Nod, and just the fact that post hoc, we have a heightened sense of self, means that we have been 'other' and now returned.

If chance favours the prepared, then surely flow follows that logic, a honed and practiced mindset, deep curiosity, and a courage to endeavour bring us to being more flowful in our everyday lives.

So, instead of accepting this perfect storm requirement, after the exhilarating moments have passed, we take a different tack and are deeply attentive and asked, 'if my optimal flow in that moment was 10, what am I feeling now?' If we were attentive to the 'normal' flowfulness of our lives, 37 trillion cells vibrating and pulsating, oozing life and flow, we would be closer to owning our flow and recognising it for what it is, a way of being that enables our endeavours and expression, instead of capitulating to the idea that flow can only be experienced in the way that it has been objectively appropriated.

To reiterate what Kotler says above, there seems to be some scientific thinking around the neurobiological prerequisites of flow, 'endorphins are definitely part of flow's cocktail and, as other researchers have determined, so are norepinephrine, dopamine, anandamide, and serotonin', and these chemicals exist in babies, present almost from the beginning. They are present in the womb, and could it be argued that if the baby is born at full term, having endured one of life's most daunting journeys and is well and mother is well, then they have experienced flow at some level; being. Optimum performance in the womb was to take on enough fuel and oxygen through the biological marvel of nature and leave at the appropriate time.

Remember the word 'subjective'. It means that you own your flow. It means that you construe your own flow scale and that you can move up or down it by being attentive to it. It's what's happening when an athlete trains for an event, or a team is searching for the perfect play, or a professional speaker prepares to give an important and interesting presentation. They are looking for opportunities to practise their flow. They are curating their life to enable them, at a specific moment in time, 'to be in the zone or be in flow', so why do we think they are not in flow whilst moving towards it,; flow is how we get there. Remember my daughter learning to drive; she was moving her flow.

Jeff Grout, former managing director of Robert Half International, the largest specialist international recruitment company in the world at the time, former business manager to Rugby World Cup winning coach, Sir Clive Woodward, and international keynote speaker of some experience, talks about getting ready to give a keynote address. He mentioned the idea that prior to going on stage, he still has butterflies, and what he notices is that about two minutes into his talk, all the 'butterflies' are flying in sync, alignment: He is in flow.

Moving up a scale, a notch, people in all walks of life are incrementally moving towards the desired flow of peak performance, and in that training, they are preparing, at the best of their ability, with a prepared mind and access to remembering and retrieval, to meet their best selves.

The internal/external reality mismatch that is faced when people talk about flow, especially coaches, is that they believe that flow is binary. I notice, as I am writing that sentence, what I believe is that to construe flow in that way perpetuates the myth that flow is a state to get into, when we seem to continually demonstrate otherwise.

The chemicals exist; the experience of flow is declared 'subjective'; one can recall and recognise moments when one flourished. Science can allegedly declare when we are in flow but has no name for 'not-flow'. Kotler, in the same article, goes on to say that

> Over the past decade, scientists have made enormous progress on flow. Advancements in brain imaging technologies have allowed us to apply serious metrics where once was only subjective experience. The state emerges from a radical alteration in normal brain function. In flow, as attention heightens the slower and energy-expensive extrinsic system, (conscious processing) is swapped out for the far faster and more efficient processing of the subconscious, intrinsic system.

And he goes on to quote Arne Deitrich, neuroscientist from the American University in Beirut. '"It's an efficiency exchange", "We're trading energy usually used for higher cognitive functions for heightened attention and awareness"'. But what if you have been able to do both before science told you, you couldn't. This is a kind of a corollary mentioned earlier Ranadivé and Maney (2011, p. 48) were hypothesising in *The Two Second Advantage*, 'The person in a state of flow is firing complex chunks so rapidly and seamlessly that she feels like she can see what's going to happen before it happens and can act with complete certainty and confidence'.

And it is worth pausing for just a moment to think about the word 'sub-conscious', meaning the part of the mind that can influence our feelings or actions, but I much prefer Alan Watts' notion that it is 'super-conscious', able to process and scan and sieve at enormous rates and then can still influence. To make conscious a positive, super, instead of a negative, instead of sub, perhaps?

So, whilst the application of brain imaging and metrics can alert us to what is going on in the brain – the brain is to biology what the mind is to consciousness, remember – what the construing mind experiences will still be subjective. We are still measuring the subjective experience of the flow state and if that is the case, who is to say when that is optimum?

As stated throughout, where we are attentive, what we are paying attention to, and how we are paying attention, is key to unlocking the trickle of flow and turning it into the torrent.

Science can measure the outputs of brain activity, but cannot measure the mind's flow inputs; how can it, it's within the domain of the individual, their consciousness, the elements in the diagram 5.1 earlier in the book, to decide when and how they will notice their mindset and then decide what way of being they will engage in to experience more.

And the more they experience, the more, again by definition, flow activity becomes the output, works its way *through* the activity, produces the painting, the fast lap time, the brilliant TED talk, or the gorgeous dress design. The flow output becomes a flow input.

Perhaps it answers the question, 'Is flow an expression of our life force living through our daily being?'. I believe it is and there is no science to disprove this, only subjective opinion.

Summary

In this chapter, we contemplate:

- 'Flow was a black box, an astoundingly intriguing phenomenon accessible only through subjective recall', according to Stephen Kotler.
- Endorphins are considered a part of flow's cocktail, as are norepinephrine, dopamine, anandamide, and serotonin.
- Where flow is if it isn't there all the time? No one has answered this successfully, so it's either a problem to be solved or a mystery to be wondered at, at least for the foreseeable future.
- Flow is perhaps so much more than a chemically induced by-product of response to the release of brain altering chemicals.
- Recognise times when you have been in 'flow'. Then you are construing your own flow reality.
- Peak or optimal performance can be considered more a measure of accomplishment, according to Jackson.
- When people talk about flow, especially coaches and commentators, flow is binary; flow or not flow.
- Science, specifically positive psychology, has no name for 'not-flow'.
- Brain imaging and metrics can alert us to what is going on in the brain, but what the construing mind experiences will still be subjective.

Exercise/Reflective Practice

1 Consider what comes first – flow to release chemicals or chemicals to induce flow?
2 Do you notice yourself in flow watching someone else in flow?
3 Is there some kind of vicarious or collaborative flow available to us, especially in teams or groups, perhaps communities?
4 If you can recognise times when you have been in 'flow', then you are construing your own flow reality. Can you recall *any* flow experience and bring it to mind?
5 Do you notice where or when flow is absent? And can you identify what exists in its place?
6 Consider the question 'if my optimal flow in that moment was 10, what am I feeling now?'.

Interview Highlights and Insights from Claire Kimber, BANT Registered Nutritional Therapist and Coach, and Clinical Supervisor (Full Disclosure, We Are Married, and Claire Is a Flow Advocate)

- Your brain is an incredibly voracious organ – an area of high metabolic activity and a high turnover of nutrients. It uses around 20% of the calories you consume, even at rest, to function well.
- Roughly a third of that calorific energy is used to rejuvenate the brain and clear away damaged proteins and cells. Every thought you have, movement you make, and sense you use (sight, sound, taste, smell, and touch) requires the neurons in your brain to work and this demands a lot of fuel and nutrients.
- It stands to reason you need to feed your brain effectively and here are some of my favourite foods for optimising your flow:
- Water: You are mostly made of water with an average of roughly 60%; however, your brain mass is about three-quarters water. When that level dips, even a little, it can result in sluggishness, fatigue, brain fog, poor reasoning/decision-making, headaches, sleep problems, and low mood. So, staying hydrated can really help with focus and mental performance and flow.
- Brain boosting omega-3 fats: If you remove water from your brain, you are left with approximately 60% fat. Your brain cell membranes are made up of fat and they determine how efficiently messages get through from one cell to another – the myelin sheaths which surround every one of your neurons is 75% fat! And essential fatty acids are important as they can't be made in the human body, and therefore you have to eat them.
- They come in a number of sizes: Omega-6 and brain-boosting omega-3. Omega-3 is associated with increased brain performance and executive function, affecting our decision-making, self-control, attention, and therefore our flow.
- Omega-6 is pro-inflammatory, meaning that it can cause inflammation. This is actually a necessary part of the immune system. The promotion of the inflammatory response through Omega-6 is essential to halt damage and promote repair. However, issues arise when the amounts of these fats that we consume are out of balance – a possible flow friction.
- The richest dietary source of omega-3 in the EPA (eicosapentaenoic acid) and DHA (docosahexaenoic acid) form, is oily fish, so eating 2–3 times per week will help. Oily fish include sardines, mackerel, anchovies, salmon, and herring (I remember them by SMASH!).
- You can also get omega-3 from plants such as flaxseeds, pumpkins, hemp, chia seeds, some seaweeds, and walnuts. For me, walnut is a wonder nut – 65% fat and 20% protein; also high in vitamin E, which is an antioxidant and helps with reducing free-radical damage in the brain, as well as vitamin B6, which is needed for serotonin (our happy neurotransmitter!), a flow essential.

- Enjoy natural fats such as butter, olive oil, and coconut oil. My favourite is the staple of the Mediterranean diet, extra virgin olive oil (EVOO), which is a pure unrefined oil made from the first 'virgin' press of the olive fruit. No heat is used in the extraction process, preserving beneficial plant compounds called polyphenols. These antioxidant compounds provide well-known benefits against heart disease and some cancers.
- Protein is the backbone of your brain cells and neurotransmitters. When we eat protein, it's digested into amino acids. There are 21 amino acids, 12 can be manufactured by the body but 9 are essential, which means they must be obtained through diet. Amino acids are the raw materials needed to make our brain cells and neurotransmitters. Examples include tyrosine, the building block of dopamine, without which we wouldn't be able to maintain focus or be productive and motivated, and another, tryptophan, needed to make serotonin, our feel-good neurotransmitter, helping us to stay calm, happy, and optimistic. All are flow essentials.
- Not all carbs are bad – you need them for sustained energy and focus and your body actually needs carbohydrates to help absorb and utilise protein properly. It is our Western diet which has resulted in many carbohydrates we consume being 'refined'. The process of refining strips away the fibres; the heat destroys the important vitamins and also changes the structure of natural oils. What is left is a refined carbohydrate that is quickly digested and absorbed. The higher the fibre your food contains, the longer it will release energy into your bloodstream and help maintain balanced blood sugar.
- Your body is programmed to keep blood sugar levels within a specific range. Eating high levels of sugary foods and refined carbohydrates leads to a spike in blood sugar, which generates the release of the hormone insulin. The role of insulin is to remove the excess sugar from the blood and send it to the liver to be stored (glycogen). If your sugar levels are high, these storage vessels may be already full; so any excess sugar will be stored as fat. Insulin isn't able to carefully calculate how much sugar to remove to restore the balance; it just hoovers up the whole lot, so that in a short period, your blood-sugar levels fall. The higher the spike in insulin, the greater the crash in blood sugar.
- When your blood sugar is low, friction in Born to Flow terms can be generated; you feel tired, irritable, anxious, shaky, headachy, dizzy, and absolutely desperate for a pick-me-up. Sugar is the body's primary source of energy, which is why the stress hormones cortisol and adrenaline are released to redress the balance. They will send a message to the liver, instructing it to release the stored sugar into the bloodstream. Cortisol also generates powerful cravings for sugary foods and stimulants like coffee. This is a double whammy as just as your liver releases the sugar stores, you'll grab a sugary snack and instead of settling back within the required range, your blood sugar will spike and the whole process will start all over again.

- It is easy for your blood sugar levels to rollercoaster over the course of the day, which means that your adrenal glands are continually releasing stress hormones, resulting in more flow friction.
- You can see why balancing your blood sugar level is key to maintaining focus and flow during the day.
- Fibre and complex carbohydrates: Your gut is home to trillions of bacterial cells which make up a unique ecosystem called the gut microbiome. Far from being unwelcomed invaders in your body, it's recognised they play a crucial role in your immune health, digestion, nutrient production, detoxification, and their activities also influence your brain. So, they are crucial for your flow well-being.
- Introduce natural probiotics and prebiotics: Fermented foods like quality 'live' yoghurt, kefir, miso, tempeh, and sauerkraut contain healthy bacteria that promote a more diverse gut microbiome. Kombucha is a fermented green or black tea; however, many shop-bought kombuchas are high in sugar (22 g of sugar or more) or may contain sugar substitutes which you may wish to avoid. Jonny Wilkinson's Living No. 1 kombucha is sugar-free and fits well with his absolute devotion to optimum performance and well-being.
- Adding prebiotic foods, such as onion, garlic, leek, apple, and artichoke, help your healthy bacteria flourish.
- Eat the rainbow: It is important that we eat a wide variety of fruits, vegetables, and salads each day to provide the key vitamins, minerals, and antioxidants needed not only to help your brain perform certain tasks but also for the functioning of your whole body and to enable optimum flow.
- Chocolate, specifically dark chocolate, stimulates all major brain chemicals of flow – dopamine, serotonin, endorphins, and anandamide. Dark chocolate is more nourishing for the gut microbiome, lower in sugar and richer in micronutrients and antioxidants. Using 85% cocoa can be a good idea; a small-scale study in 2022 found that it can beneficially modulate the gut microbiome with associated mental health benefits, by definition, flow benefits.
- Coffee is a good source of polyphenols and antioxidants which help reduce inflammation and promote health. However, as it contains caffeine, it is a stimulant directly affecting the brain and central nervous system with an immediate boosting effect on neurotransmitters, for example, it increases dopamine, providing focus, motivation, and alertness. However, too much dopamine can cause anxiety and agitation for long term, thereby causing less flow. Caffeine becomes a problem when it's used too often or at the wrong time of day (in the evening, for instance). Caffeine is a sleep disruptor and by definition, your flow recovery is altered.
- Adenosine is a chemical that builds up in your body the longer you are awake, which makes you feel sleepier. Caffeine blocks adenosine receptors, fooling your body into thinking it is not tired when it comes to bedtime, making you feel wired and tired!
- As a nutritionist, my belief in the power of food to enable flow is unshakable.

Reference

Jackson, S. A., Thomas, P. R., Marsh, H. W., & Smethurst, C. J. (2001). Relationships between flow, self-concept, psychological skills, and performance. *Journal of Applied Sport Psychology*, *13*(2), 129–153.

Ranadivé, V., & Maney, K. (2011). *The two-second advantage: How we succeed by anticipating the future–just enough.* Crown Publishing Group.

Chapter 10

Remembering Flow

Anabranch

What does excellence look like if you can't see the scoreboard, or you don't know or quite understand the data? It's fairly easy to imagine that excellence looks like flow made real, whether by a relay team in full flight or a murmuration of starlings. The key to this effortless effort is underpinned by standard operating protocols (SOPs) that have either been taught or naturally learnt through endless hours of being and practice.

To clarify that society can repress and hinder the development of flow, the paradox is that when we wake up to this fact and wish to perform together effectively, we have to remember, recognise, and relearn how to increase our innate flow and we have to train and practise for our excellence.

Paradoxically we have to work hard to achieve the effortless effort, which emerges once again from a natural capability and capacity for flow. As Martha Graham said, 'It takes at least five years of rigorous training to be spontaneous'. What she had forgotten is that spontaneity was present in her childhood and drummed out of her, as described earlier by Charles Hazlehurst.

The memory and the ability to remember seemed to me, from the beginning of thinking about flow, to play a crucial role in one's ability to construe what flow means to us as individuals. Steven Pinker said on *"How Do Nature and Nurture Combine to Make Us Who We Are?"* (on NPR / TED Radio Hour) 'Kids come into the world with certain temperaments and talents, it doesn't all come from the outside'.

When one examines the way that science breaks down memory, it may be no coincidence that we forget we are born to flow. Just a quick glance at what the all-knowing Google machine reveals, in no particular order; short-term and long-term memory, episodic and emotional memory, semantic, autobiographical, declarative, working, explicit and implicit memory, and sensory and visual memory, I could go on, but your flow might be somewhat impeded, and you would not remember them.

As we have seen it is easy to drift into what lies beneath the bonnet of the brain, what the mind thinks of itself, if it is just consciousness that is in flow, and if that consciousness knows what it is when it flows, and so on, but the purpose of this book is not to take the reader on a tour of the brain and its functions, it is closer to what the eminent Zen scholar Suzuki writes in the foreword to one of my often referred to books, a touchstone for my thinking if you will and mentioned earlier,

DOI: 10.4324/9781351169929-11

Zen in the Art of Archery by Herrigel et al. (1953, p. 81), 'Man is a thinking reed but his great works are done when he is not calculating and thinking. Childlikeness (sic) has to be restored after long years of training in the art of self-forgetfulness'.

And Justin Hughes, former Red Arrows pilot when asked about whether he thought, as a child, he would have had more flow experiences,

> I think that generally, children have more flow experiences than adults by probably a massive factor. Less constraints, less worry about the consequences, or other people's opinions. They're just getting the reward from being in the moment and having a great time.

When asked if he'd ever tried to replicate it, it was evident that he hadn't considered that he could: He had no need to encode it as a child and so had forgotten about those experiences.

One of the effects of the long years of conforming and performing to societal expectations and norms is the forgetting of flow as 'a way of being'. As I have previously suggested, the child's natural predisposition is one of flow, the first step, therefore, is to remember and more specifically to remember your sublime experiences of flow as early in your childhood as you can.

This should be easily achievable according to a thought in an article in Scientific American by James Broadway, post-doctoral researcher in the department of psychological and brain sciences at UCL, quoting Claudia Hammond,

> From childhood to early adulthood, we have many fresh experiences and learn countless new skills. As adults, though, our lives become more routine, and we experience fewer unfamiliar moments. As a result, our early years tend to be relatively overrepresented in our autobiographical memory and, on reflection, seem to have lasted longer.

You may also consider the idea of 'collective' or 'collaborative' flow as an aide-memoire, the point at which you were completely in sync with another, perhaps a close friend who you shared an interest or childhood passion with – one who you can remember being completely at ease with, and at the same time oblivious to the world around you as you engaged in the 'art' and flowfulness of 'being' a child. Imaginations conjoined, direction of thought unspoken, but acknowledged and understood. Time was the river that you and your friend flowed along, just as you flowed along with each other's ideas and games, knowing what each other was thinking and going to do next: synergy in flow.

Perhaps later in the day, flowing, you retold the story of your day to those who would listen, encode, and consolidate it, ready for retrieval at a later date. As you recall such days, you will also recall how the day stretched out and seemed endless, that the summers were warmer or the winters had more snow, you may remember the ease and endless energy associated with that experience. You may recognise a 'feeling' that is evoked in you by simply remembering your flow experience, your uninhibited way of being and expressing in the world, and your curiosity in engaging with it.

Fully associating with your flow experience may enable you to start to reconnect in a real way with the power of living life in flow and if you have recognised, remembered, and recalled such a moment, you may appreciate that it was a 'deep' flow experience and that your life has since had greater or lesser experiences of flow, but that it has been a constant companion.

The art of self-forgetfulness is lost in the moment when we stop daring and start caring, as it were and where once we roamed free, if only in our imagination, unfettered and unrestrained by the communities and social norms that come to dominate us. We start to construe ourselves as different if we don't comply and conform. We start to care about how we 'fit' into the boxes that we have been shown, follow the examples that have been set; we start to inhibit our flow growth by the need to belong without necessarily understanding what we will belong to. We start to compare and as Teddy Roosevelt said, 'Comparison is the thief of joy', it may also be the thief of your flow.

Why then do we fail to encode flow as we are living with it, being it, and learning it? I think we may fail to encode flow into our memory as a way of being in the world simply because we have no reason; we don't know what we don't know. Our minds are so rapidly overwhelmed by the leviathan force of coercive societies that we quickly become complicit and compliant, and we do the number one thing we assume will help us to get on in the world we conform.

Because we do not encode flow as a way of being in the world, retrieval becomes more difficult, which is strange given the over-representation in autobiographical memory as described earlier by Claudia Hammond; but as stated a moment ago, we don't know what we don't know.

There may be an exception, and that is for those who find their métier in life early, whether they are called to sport or the humanities, maths, or science. Something happens when one discovers a passion wants to express itself through our lives. Perhaps that calling to express ourselves fully is one gateway to owning our flow early in life; to follow your bliss, as Joseph Campbell was fond of saying.

However, if flow, as an explanatory principle, is a part of our evolutionary make-up, our biology, our consciousness, like intuition or the epiphany, and perhaps in the not-too-distant future if this idea will be more widely accepted, then retrieving even the fleeting glimpses of flow should be possible through heightened awareness of those moments, practice, and sciences.

Summary

In this chapter, we have thought about:

- It's fairly easy to imagine that excellence looks like flow made real.
- Society can repress and hinder the development of flow.

- The key to this effortless effort is underpinned by SOPs that have either been taught or naturally learnt through endless hours of being and practice.
- Martha Graham said, 'It takes at least five years of rigorous training to be spontaneous'.
- 'Kids come into the world with certain temperaments and talents, it doesn't all come from the outside' according to Steven Pinker.
- Generally four types of memory are considered:

  Working memory to store information for short periods
  Episodic memory to recall past events – fresh or distant
  Semantic memory to remember the meanings of words or facts
  Prospective memory to plan

- Our early years tend to be relatively overrepresented in our autobiographical memory.
- Fully associating with your flow experience may enable you to start to reconnect in a real way with the power of living life in flow.
- The art of self-forgetfulness is encapsulated in the moment when we stop daring and start caring.
- 'Comparison is the thief of joy'. I would suggest this is especially true for younger people in the age of social media, where comparison is a dominant force.
- We may fail to encode flow into our memory as a way of being in the world simply because we have no reason; we don't know what we don't know.

Exercise/Reflective Practice

1 Martha Graham said, 'It takes at least five years of rigorous training to be spontaneous'. Where do you think you are most spontaneous? Does it come from being authentic, in trying to please or conform or is it latent potential emerging as an action?
2 'Kids come into the world with certain temperaments and talents, it doesn't all come from the outside', said Steven Pinker. What temperaments do you recognise in yourself or in others whom you interact with?
3 As you reflect on moments where you have compared yourself to others, do you find that it has enabled or impeded your flow?
4 Does comparison, especially in the competitive arena, elevate your flow? Does it enable you in some way or does it cause interference?
5 As an adult, as you reflect on your life both pre- and post-18 years of age, what do you find easier to remember or recall?
6 Is it easier to remember flow like moments from your preteen or teen years?

References

Herrigel, E., Hull, R. F. C., & Blum, R. (1953). *Zen in the art of archery*. Pantheon Books.
Pinker, S. (1997). *How the mind works*. W. W. Norton.

Chapter 11

In the Groove

Currents

There comes a point at which one must stop tinkering and ask, what if I am experiencing flow each day and don't understand or recognise what's going on?

'Stop tinkering' comes from a conversation Nile Rodgers, one of the most successful record producers in recent history, had when he appeared on Desert Island Discs in 2018, a radio show in the UK. He was asked how he knew a track was complete and was as good as it could be. His answer was simple, and in some ways, enlightening from someone who is a consummate perfectionist; 'after you have done all you can do you have to let the people decide, you have to stop tinkering and let the song out in public'.

I think this is akin to the Watts' idea earlier,

> In every art one comes to realise there is a point where your will is exhausted, you've tried everything to make something work & it won't work, and then to achieve the perfection of the art, something has to happen of itself, which we variously call grace, inspiration or tariki.

It shows a confidence in your own ability to trust yourself, to know you have done all you can do, and you need to move on, to get out of your own way. The 'tinkering' word strikes home as something that most of us have experienced during our lives, with diet, or training, or study or a work project; we tinker, when in actuality, we know two things that are diametrically opposed, we must either make radical change to generate the change we want or we must stop tinkering and stride out into the world with what we have. To find out if we are in the groove, if we are in flow, we have to let go of where we are to get to where we could be, or as Joseph Campbell, the comparative mythologist, said, 'We must be willing to get rid of the life we've planned, so as to have the life that is waiting for us'– maybe a life with flow.

The idea that we should wait for these magic flow moments, only treat them in a post hoc sense, and only recognise them after the event, is one of the great barriers to human performance reaching optimal levels. Awareness of your mindset, beyond being mindful of it, to act, to increase the skill, enjoyment, and engagement with the moment, and to impact your environment so that in the next moment you

DOI: 10.4324/9781351169929-12

are increasing your flow rate, is the optimal way to engage with your best self. We increase our flow to meet our better selves.

The phrase 'in the groove' seems to come close to describing, in an idiomatic sense, the idea of being in the best/most flow you can be. The origin of this phrase seems to coincide with two events in the early 20th century, the arrival of the phonograph and then quickly spreading through the colloquialism of the jazz age. With the advent of the phonograph, users were instructed to put the needle accurately into the groove to achieve the best sound quality. If the needle was slightly out of the groove, sound quality deteriorated; precisely, in the groove meant better sound. So it was that the phrase was quickly used to describe jazz musicians and dancers in the swinging twenties who were in the groove, feeling the pace and rhythm of the music; interestingly, there is also a feedback loop inasmuch as the audience feels the groove too. Slightly out of the groove a sound would still be heard, but with the needle in the groove, a whole new sound was available. An alignment needed to take place.

Could this be how it is with flow that sometimes the needle is in the groove and at other times not so much? Not only do you hear the difference, but you feel it, and the music of life, of being, is still playing, at least till the end of our own unique record.

This analogy seems to me to be pertinent and hold some weight because of the human condition as much as anything else. Our inner selves battle continually between what Tim Gallwey describes as 'self 1' and 'self 2'; Gallwey's answer was to shift focus to the voice of self 2 and whilst switching focus requires great effort, it is also a false positive because it is merely asking you to focus attention on one 'inner voice' instead of the 'other'. However, the Inner Game is one of the best positive psychology tools out there, so it should be explored too.

The born to flow hypothesis is not dissimilar. However, where the inner game construct of two voices requires a switch in focus, the born to flow hypothesis requires you remember that flow existed before those two voices appeared, often at the behest of the outside world that is quick to implant such voices in our heads, to judge, and to linger like an echo in long abandoned corridors of time; this is a critical distinction and resonates with James Hillman's (2017) assertion as mentioned earlier, 'They (children) are trying to live two lives at once, the one they were born with, and the one, of the place and among the people they were born into'.

An echo can be so powerful that it can often haunt people their entire lives. Is it any wonder that so many executives and leaders, site 'Imposter syndrome' as something that plagues them throughout their professional careers, they are listening to voices that may not be their own, haunted by societies latent impression on their being?

There was a time when the imposter, as a state or character in your make-up, was not available to you. There was a time when you only had access to the one 'true' voice in your head and that voice was on a mission to excel in the role of being you.

This far into the book you will have some idea of the leviathan force ranged against you from an early age, and not all of that force is intentional. So, it's not impossible to conceive why memory is so cherished by all societies around the world, by all ethnicities, by every age, creed, and colour; something is going on with memory and 'by owning your memory, owning your mind', as Antonio Damasio says, you can come closer to being in the groove and owning your flow.

If creativity likes a quiet mind according to some researchers, then emotion loves movement; it's really hard to be still and be fully emotional. In the midst of grief, we reach out or we go inside ourselves; when cheering for our team, we stand and clap and jump and cheer; when we meet an old friend at the airport, we run towards them in the same way surfers run towards ocean, to greet an old friend. So, it is with flow, it's a doing word, a moving word, a verb. And when it's used as a noun, you cannot get away from the movement contained within the word 'flow'.

'Remember' is also a verb, it requires action, engagement, and full association with the time before your flow diminished; memory is the key to unlocking so much of our lives in relation to flow and why we might have a reduced flow capability as we grow older.

It's worth noticing that when someone asks you to switch 'focus' what they are doing is sending you into recall mode; you have to remember how to switch focus and thereby summon other stuff or data around the periphery of the activity you are actually undertaking. You will see Tony Robbins in many instances asking people he is working with to change focus, to change state, to focus on a time when they were proud or excited or some other state that usually engages lots of emotional content and thus, movement. He gets them to increase 'flow' through connection with emotion and through remembering, although he says, 'switching focus'.

George Kelly (2003, p. 32) stated his fundamental postulate as, 'a person's processes are psychologically channelized by the way they anticipate events'. Again, we see the power that remembering has over how we flow or move forwards, for how can we anticipate if we don't have a memory to anticipate with? Memory is the antecedent of anticipation and the grandmother of flow.

'Flow' seems to have in it a fragility that is dependent on the fact that this way of living life has been influenced by those factors that have some hold over the way we express our life. What is it about owning our own flow and thus the key to our own peak or optimal performance that is so bothersome? Because owning your peak performance, through the acknowledgement that flow is a way to express it, is the key to exceptional outcomes in sport, business, and life.

Demonstrably peak performance is an outcome of the human being in flow; however, this is construed by the individual, as well as the gold medal or the award at work in recognition. To place a framework around what is and isn't flow, is perhaps to restrict it by saying what constitutes it, and that is to dilute the human experience of flow.

The experience of flow as a remembered event is relatively easy for most people; usually it will require a visit to a distant past, and often, as far back as a childhood encounter with life, as stated earlier. The flow that emerges during play is a contradiction to the accepted wisdom that flow requires clear goals to be achieved. When lost amid play, a child is making up and running with a narrative that is pouring forth from their imagination, the child's analysis, and synthesis of what is emerging in that moment is not predicated on some clearly defined goal.

Lego Serious Play™ has a nice expression that encapsulates this, 'construct, make meaning, tell stories'. One may argue that the goal was 'to play successfully' but the child would only, through expressing play and experimenting, understand what successful play feels like; it should not be a predetermined outcome lest the joy of discovery be ripped from hearts and minds finding their way in the world by creatively recreating their lives through the act of play.

I would argue that all the best teams, both in business and sport, establish what excellence or success looks like without the need for a scoreboard; they are committed to ways of working and being together, to the place where they work, and how they work. They have formed a way of recognising flow in their excellence that is missing in the mediocre and the average. The score is an outcome of excellence and flow, as Bill Walsh, NFL coach, said,

> A resolute and resourceful leader understands that there are a multitude of means to increase the probability of success. And that's what it all comes down to, namely, intelligently, and relentlessly seeking solutions that will increase your chance of prevailing in a competitive environment. When you do that, the score will take care of itself.
>
> (Walsh et al., 2009)

I suggest that flow is all of the above and more and exhibited in the child at play. A resolute and resourceful leader isn't born, they are learning through experimentation, through collecting and developing resource, capability, and capacity, and through play, throughout their lives.

Further, as the child understands, through their imagination, that there are a multitude of scenarios to pick from, mostly archetypal, many emerging from the early years spent watching and absorbing, analysing, and synthesising; they refine their storytelling and their plays in life and on the field. A child seeks solutions intuitively from the minute they want *to stand* in the ecosystem where they will spend the rest of their lives, and in doing all the above, they are picking up points as they go. By application the score is taking care of itself, expressing it through flow.

There is a propensity in life driven by fear that without data we are nothing; that we cannot know excellence without some kind of metric; and that the scoreboard is the supreme ruler of success. But you don't need to measure the smile after the perfect handoff in a full flowing rugby match, or the child helping the elder across the road, or the business that goes against the grain and trusts its people to be productive wherever and whenever. You can try and measure it, but 'when a measure becomes a target, it ceases to be a good measure', to quote Marilyn Strathern (1997) as she expressed Goodhart's Law.

In finding their flow, people often find their vocation, or their calling, if you will. People attentive to flow are productive, creative, and present in ways that we cannot fathom, unless you take a tape measure to their essence and as W. H. Auden in 1955 wrote,

> You need not see what someone is doing to know if it is his vocation, you only have to watch his eyes: a cook mixing a sauce, a surgeon making a primary incision, a clerk completing a bill of lading, wear that same rapt expression, forgetting themselves in function. How beautiful it is, that eye–on-the-object-look.

In creating an ecosystem that *supports* one's flow, one creates a place that survives and thrives on excellence, a place where flow can grow and express itself. But if we flip that and say that flow is not dependent on the ecosystem, but the ecosystem is dependent on the flow that is present in it to continue to thrive, one starts to create a virtuous spiral, as shown in Figure 11.1:

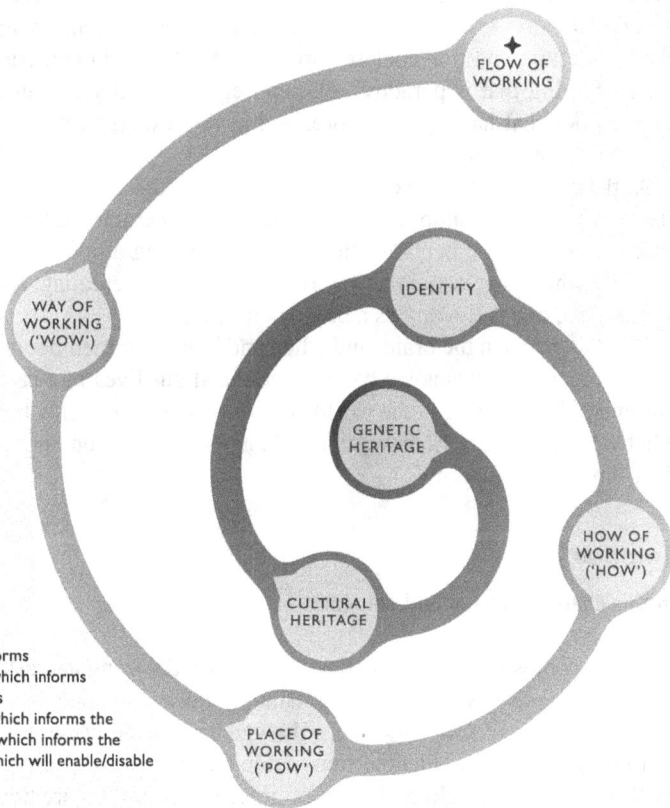

GENETIC HERITAGE informs
CULTURAL HERITAGE which informs
IDENTITY which informs
HOW one might work which informs the
PLACE one might work which informs the
WAY one might work which will enable/disable
FLOW.
Born to Flow®

Figure 11.1 The flow of work. A spiral

If we are born with traits and dispositions, as Steven Pinker suggests, and they are melded with our cultural heritage, which in the ecosystem start to form identity, you are probably learning how to work your way through the world. This will inform, and you will be informed by, the place where working takes place and ultimately produce ways of working with flow. I have assumed momentarily that 'flow' is a part of our genetic heritage. I suggest, strongly, that owning your flow is to own your peak performance.

One thing that people with high levels of flow in their lives seem to do is remember, recognise, reorder, and reorientate around people, places, task, and activities quicker and with more resolve.

Each of those 'r' words seem to indicate a notion of adaptation and mobility of thought, through high levels of engagement and participation in life, and the reward chemicals that the body and brain are hardwired to deliver, as we are collecting meaningful and significant experiences, are enablers.

Creation is a synthesis of ideas, things, moments, or people coming together at a point in time, that enables flow to come more to the forefront of cognitive experience and thus produce something at one end of the scale, even if, for example, it is the creation of the perfect ride on a surfboard. Person, board, leash, seabed, wind direction, and tide coalesce around a synthesised expression of life producing something that is paradoxically, entirely new and yet is an approximation of all the rides that have gone before, and in this example, there is usually a smile somewhere on the way.

At the other end of the scale, we may find that those 'r' words are still at play in creating the weekly shop, walking through the supermarket, buying necessities for survival or the ingredients for thriving, and cooking a new and delicious recipe – one is synthesising, remembering, reorganising re-orientating, and reordering, and in doing so, one is flowing as a being in motion.

What happens in the brain, and when and how we remember is the key. The subjective recall that means we have experienced our lives in a certain way, through our internal construing of the world, also means that the ability to remember shapes what we will do next, how we will do it, and depending on our recall, how we will flow through the activity.

Summary

In this chapter, we see and consider:

- There comes a point at which one must stop tinkering and ask, am I experiencing flow each day and not understanding it or recognising what's going on?
- 'After you have done all you can do, you have to let the people decide, you have to stop tinkering and let the song out in public'.
- What if Watts is right and tariki or grace or inspiration are flow manifestations. 'In every art one comes to realise there is a point where your will is exhausted, you've tried everything to make something work & it won't work, and then to

achieve the perfection of the art, something has to happen of itself, which we variously call grace, inspiration or tariki'.

- Joseph Campbell, the comparative mythologist, said, 'We must be willing to get rid of the life we've planned, so as to have the life that is waiting for us'.
- 'They (children) are trying to live two lives at once, the one they were born with, and the one, of the place and among the people they were born into', so says James Hillman. We are making it so much harder to retain flow after childhood if we are setting up life in this way.
- 'By owning your memory, owning your mind', according to Antonio Damasio.
- The ability to remember and fully associate with the memory is key to enhancing one's flow.
- The experience of flow as a remembered experience is relatively easy for most people; usually it will require a visit to a distant past, and often, as far back as a childhood encounter with life.
- A resolute and resourceful leader isn't born, they learn through experimentation, through collecting and developing resource, capability, and capacity, and through play, throughout their lives.
- 'When a measure becomes a target, it ceases to be a good measure' according to Marilyn Strathern.
- In creating an ecosystem that *supports* a person's flow, one creates a place that survives and thrives on excellence, a place where flow can grow and express itself.
- Owning your flow is to own your peak performance.
- One thing that people with high levels of flow in their lives seem to do is remember, recognise, reorder, and reorientate around people, places, task, and activities quicker and with more resolve.

Exercise/Reflective Practice

1 What are you still tinkering with that you should let go out into the world and find its own way?
2 Have you ever felt like you were an imposter and if so, what do you think contributed to that feeling the most? And, if you have never felt like an imposter, what have you built your identity on?

References

Auden, W. H. (2015). *W. H. Auden: Prose, Volume III, 1949–1955* (E. Mendelson, Ed.). Faber & Faber.
Hillman, J. (2017). *The soul's code: In search of character and calling.* Ballantine Books.
Kelly, G. (2003). *The psychology of personal constructs: Volume one.* Routledge.
Strathern, M. (1997). 'Improving ratings': Audit in the British University system. *European Review, 5*(3), 305–321.
Walsh, B., Jamison, S., & Walsh, C. (2009). *The score takes care of itself: My philosophy of leadership.* Penguin.

Chapter 12

Flow Alteration

Dams

In a deeply axiomatic way, flow is ever present, and the key is in the remembering and becoming constantly and consistently aware of your flow. The fact that we forget about flow is self-evidently true and given the way memory works, and what it needs to cope with, throughout a lifetime, it's not surprising that we don't encode it for retrieval. There's simply no need at the time when flow may be strongest and unfettered in our lives, to contemplate it becoming a backwater to our success.

For some people, this is an occasional forgetting; their performances drift from high to low without any real contemplation or reflection on what they are experiencing because we are simply not taught or encouraged to reflect on this 'force' emergent within us. There is no room for embodied cognition that from the beginning in our lives, flow arises from our bodily interactions with the world we inhabit, which is an emergent property, perhaps based on the way we feel before we think.

For others, it is a complete forgetting, a total lack of awareness that flow is present, and again, there is no need to feel that life might change, as our flow is constantly assailed by almost immeasurable forces that will rail against us during the course of our lives.

By 'a lack of awareness' I'm thinking of how we might otherwise categorise the flow experience: A 'magical' walk in the woods, loss of self in writing a poem, or an ecstatic experience. This suggests that it is worth looking at why we forget our flow, and at the major forces that constrict or diminish it, as there can hardly be an evolutionary advantage to forgetting.

In constricting or diminishing flow, there are two big actors: The individual themselves and the communities that we inhabit. We will look at the second first, as it may be the primary actor, as mentioned earlier.

'Communities' is in the plural because you typically belong to a number of communities concurrently and they all have their own pressures, stressors, and benefits: Family, clan, tribe, nation, social media platform and group, club, political party, church, professional body, and work organisation – all of these exist within a much larger ecosystem, and interestingly they will all have the power to impact your flow.

In order to be accepted into a community – to survive and thrive – we are required to fit in, to play by the rules, and to imitate. And other more senior members

DOI: 10.4324/9781351169929-13

of the community have a number of tools to ensure that we do. At the more positive end, this might be about the provision of rewards or benefits, access to resources, or giving encouragement and positive feedback. At the more negative end, it might be about the withdrawal of rewards and benefits, about punishments, shaming people, or simply ignoring them. This process of socialisation is most often in relation to children, but it continues throughout our lives and endeavours.

Socialisation is a force that acts on us. Some of which may well be for our own good, for example, sharing toys so that we learn and are capable of creating adult relationships in later life. The force may also be for the 'benefit' of others.

John D. Rockefeller, who founded the General Education Board in the United States of America, joined later in the endeavour by Andrew Carnegie, was perhaps not as interested in liberating people through education as might be expected from what appears as a grand philanthropic gesture, but rather it could be suggested that he was concerned with building a workforce of reliable, predictable, and compliant citizens to 'man' the factories, the world of commerce in that trinity of power, Rockefeller, Carnegie, and education.

There may be some doubt to the validity of this view, but the somewhat amazing aspect of this is that Rockefeller seemed to be clear and explicit in his intent. Frederick T. Gates, president of the General Education Board wrote,

> In our dream, we have limitless resources, and the people yield themselves with perfect docility to our moulding hand. The present educational conventions fade from our minds; and, unhampered by tradition, we work our good upon a grateful and responsive rural folk.

There is no doubt that they understood that this docile, compliant workforce could increase Rockefeller and Carnegie's power and bank balance. A counter argument might be that these two titans of commerce looked upon the docile rural folk with benevolence and decided that they could do more to enable them; the language, albeit from a different era, seems to indicate that this is unlikely, 'the people yield themselves with perfect docility to our moulding hand'.

In fairness then, we must quote a phrase that Gates writes towards the end of his thinking, and reiterate that he was thinking about rural schooling,

> So we have brought our little community at last to art and refinement. Such a people will demand literature and a library of their own. And when they begin to select and to read good books for themselves, our particular task will be done. We may leave them then, I think, to their natural local leaders. We have taught them how to live the life of the farm, of the fireside, of the rural community, to make it healthful, intelligent, efficient, productive, social, and no longer isolated. We have wakened *sluggishness to interest and inquiry.* (my italics). We have given the mind, in the intelligent conduct of the daily vocation, in the study and enjoyment of nature, material for some of the joys of the intellectual life. We have trained the eye for beauty, the ear for harmony, the soul for gentleness

and courtesy, and made possible to these least of Christ's brethren the life of love and joy and admiration. We have made country life more desirable than city life and raised up in the country the natural aristocracy of the nation.

As I read this, it still rings of someone else knowing what is best for 'other', by definition to commandeer their flow.

How we are complicit in our own compliance is ably demonstrated in a famous comic sketch first broadcast on BBC1, 'The Frost Report' in 1966 on British TV. It is satire of the British Class system featuring John Cleese, Ronnie Barker, and Ronnie Corbett, representing the upper, middle, and lower classes, respectively. Suitably, John Cleese is very tall and dressed in appropriate identifying 'uniform', that of bowler hatted, pinstriped city worker typical of Britain in the 1960s; Barker, in the middle, is adorned in a trilby and off-the-peg suit, a member of the 'vulgar' middle classes; and Corbett, the shortest, is attired in working men's clothes.

Before they speak, we have insight into identity, station in life, and the compliance to the system. It is remarkable how it deconstructs the class, education, and workplace of the time in 1 minute and 49 seconds.

Cleese,	'I look down on him because I am upper class'.
Barker says,	'I look up to him because he is upper class, but I look down on him because he is lower class'.
Corbett responds,	*'I know my place'.*

However, there is a slight wrinkle when Cleese admits to having, 'innate breeding, but no money' and Barker still capitulates to the alleged status of the 'taller man'. You can find it on YouTube.

Being compliant and complicit in this way maintains the status quo that Rockefeller and Carnegie may have been after and demonstrates the way in which identity is assumed and therefore can impede or alter flow.

Summary

In this chapter, we consider:

- Given the complexity of our lives, and the way our lives are structured in some parts of the world, it's not surprising that we don't encode flow for retrieval; we don't know that we will forget that we need it. Further, if it is part of our being we might not even recognise it, like an unconscious bias, it remains unconscious until deep exploration takes place.
- We are not often taught or encouraged to *reflect* on any 'force' that may be emergent within us, whether flow, self-reliance, self-concept, resilience, mental toughness etc. These are relatively new as subjects for study.
- There is no evolutionary advantage to forgetting we are born to flow; like many things, creativity, for example, we are 'told' we are not X and we should

consider Y. When the sum total of our being is not fully emergent in the world, we are already being conditioned by what 'others' think of us.

- In diminishing or altering flow, there are two big actors: You, the individual, and the communities that you inhabit. And these alterations can be concurrent and overloading, which in turn can overwhelm.
- We typically belong to a number of communities concurrently and they all have their own pressures, stressors, and benefits.
- In order to be accepted into a community we are, in some way, required to fit in. And we can fit in, even if we don't, as the community labels us so we fit into the eco-system as an outcast; paradoxically.
- Socialisation is a force that acts on us (for better or worse).

Exercise/Reflective Practice

1 Consider how flow feels rather than how you think it feels (there is a difference)?
2 Reflect on how many alterations might occur during the course of your day. For example, when you wake, do you wake into the moment, or perhaps into the future of what the day holds or do you replay something from the previous day's activity?
3 Reflect on whether you have been able to identify a feeling of flow as embodied in your consciousness or whether it has completely vanished in the act of forgetting.
4 As you prepare for bed, going through your usual routine, whatever that may be, take time to reflect of any flow moment that was emergent in your day. You may aid this exercise by forgetting you are trying to remember; meditative breathing might assist this.

Interview Insights and Highlights from Jonny Wilkinson Entrepreneur, Former England Fly Half, World Cup Winner

- (Thinking about flow) 'One (thing) is that it's almost like a trance like state, whereby the question and the answer kind of arise at the same time, you recognise what you need, and at the same time, what you want, or what is needed, at the same time that what is needed appears with it. And that's the kind of crossing over the boundaries of the time and the space stuff'.
- 'I think there's also something to be said about the dissolution or the disappearance of the boundary between you and what you're doing. So that oneness of it' (in flow).
- 'The energies on the outside (of us) are such a perfect match, that it almost gives the immediate impression that there's nothing in between' (the flow experience).
- (On coaching and flow) 'when I coach kickers, you're talking, you're exploring and suddenly they'll move towards a kick and its done. There, the first step in embodiment, on the first step in (towards the ball), is so pure. That I guess as

someone watching I'm also in that flow that I recognised somehow there's a perfect match (of energy)'.

- (On the flow connection) 'It's funny how I always feel that I have a role to play, in that if I step out of *my* flow, and I start thinking of reporting back (i.e. commenting on/to the kicker), it won't happen. I can actually impact that flow, but to just sit there, and just allow, but there is part of you that recognises the way someone moves into, some way that it's not just oh, I think they're looking good. It's done'.
- (How does flow fit?) 'I see to a degree flow being slightly irrational, not just slightly, I probably see flow being very irrational against the social construct we've got, because the social constructs are basically around being able to report on everything you're doing'.
- (The construct of goal setting) 'I don't think we ever choose our own goals. I think at some point, they will come through us and then we decide there's something exciting enough about them, or we could kind of, I guess, help them to keep coming through us'.
- (On visualisation) 'After a while it can become like work unless you have a relationship where you allow it to go where it wants to go. There's acceptance and allowance' (in waking up to the world and our potential).
- (On shifting energy from doing to being, for a coachee/player) 'You can often see when that voice is in charge, the limiting voice. You can see when it's in control of the posture, you can see when it's in control of the comments that are coming out, the questions coming out with the self-critique, the jerky movements, the tempo, everything, the energy there. And you can feel the shift when suddenly, the symptoms of it, *(towards just being) it* might be the conversation becomes a bit more playful or exciting, or explosive'.
- (On feelings and flow) 'I think you've got to be willing to go with them. You've got to be willing to enter that space. And that's when you come back to that childlike thing, which is that children don't know how *not* to go into that space'.
- 'I think that spontaneity, and that's slipping into the realm of who I'm supposed to be'.
- 'Evolution as opposed to self-development' (on growing as a person).
- 'Deep down, where or when someone's speaking to you, you know, if everything lines up' (on developing connection).
- 'If I move through different arenas and I'm exploring through challenge, and I "allow", there is going to be evolution and as I grow older, I have to expand, as a part of that path, I think we are built to grow and expand'.
- (On being by nature and natural flow) 'I would feel drawn to water, you know when a stream reaches a gathering point and you have the sense that this is effortlessly doing this all day, while you're sleeping, it's doing it and it does it without any complaint, and it's always a beautiful, natural un-conflicted event, so yes, I feel drawn to that'.
- (On flowing conversations) 'It's a two-way street. And I think that kind of openness, that's where I find it now open, deep, honest conversations, where

suddenly my mouth is running ahead of my brain into that space of emergence. And it's running so fast that it's exploring ahead of where I've been before, and it's going to find something. And when it finds something, along with someone else, it really, it seems to land'.

- (On cultivating growth and flow) 'Do whatever you can to trigger that entanglement, So that you can identify and disentangle'.

Chapter 13

Interrupting Flow

The Continuing Alteration of the Terrain Flow through We Flow

Compliance is one of the many factors we face in life that can interrupt, dilute, or, as mentioned previously, alter flow. Our compliance in the world is rooted in a deep psychological need to belong to 'something'.

The word, 'interrupting' has been used deliberately here because it follows that if flow is an ever-present resource for us to tap into, then we will encounter things that impede our ability to flow and interrupt it – a friction, as described, belonging to a community, for example. Of course, belonging to a community can also enhance our experience and rate of flow.

My experience, as an executive performance coach, working with elite performers in sport, leaders in business, or people just making their way in life, in their careers, is that sometimes they feel, like they are swimming against the tide, a struggle seems to ensue, as if fighting some under current. If they focus and pay attention to these ripples in the flow, perturbations if you will, very quickly they identify what may be slowing flow. Based on the simple premise – where attention goes, energy flows – placing your attention on the right thing, at the right time, can unleash energy exponentially. You can map these on your template at the back of this book.

Our conditioning, and we don't necessarily notice it, as in the Goleman quote that follows, is such that our minds are constantly interrupted, and our flow impeded by things we encounter on our journey (don't think of pink elephants, sorry!) and we could hypothesise that by a certain age, we would be used to this interference and be able to cope with it, managing our thoughts and responses to manifestations or alterations in the environment. It seems that this is a capability that we haven't fully developed, is not taught well in education, if at all, and yet what you hear constantly are people talking about how they are disrupted, lose focus and concentration, and forget where they should be placing their attention.

As McGilchrist (2018) says of attention, 'it is actually nothing less than the way in which we relate to the world'. So that's a powerful reason to be attentive to where you place your attention, it shapes your reality.

At this stage of our evolution, this seems slightly at odds with what else our species has achieved and yet, a being in flow is considered elusive and resigned to the

DOI: 10.4324/9781351169929-14

preternatural, to some sacred Valhallian Hall where only gods may partake of the flow nectar. It still seems kind of ludicrous to me.

Here's another clue, written by Daniel Goleman and often misattributed to R. D. Laing (Goleman, 1985),

> The range of what we think and do is limited by what we fail to notice, and because we fail to notice that we fail to notice, there is little we can do to change until we notice how failing to notice shapes our thoughts and deeds.

If you don't notice that you lack something, you can't improve your performance in that specific area.

When you think back on your life, whether you are 15 (not too young to be reading this, so good on you) or 65, it might be interesting to examine the binary nature of some of the things we were taught and we came to accept as the norm, the received wisdom and whilst the interrupters of your flow may not have cognisance of their actions, interrupt it they did. Here are a few binary examples that you have lodged away:

'Isn't she/he walking yet'? It ultimately requires a binary answer from the parent/carer and furthermore is a statement not a question. The adult is now processing this, perhaps with their flow interrupted, comparing and judging, and this may trickle down and interrupt the way that they engage with the child thereafter.

'Isn't she pretty?' Statement as question again, and also naming 'pretty' denotes 'ugly' as per the earlier example from the Tao Te Ching. An adult says to a child learning to walk, who is upright and moving forwards, 'who's a clever boy/girl?' denoting when one gets it wrong i.e., a fall of tumble, stupid/wrong/bad, etc. You get the point? It's a slippery slope.

Interruption of flow starts quite early and for no real reason, except perhaps that most have forgotten we have been born to flow i.e., we interrupt another's flow because we have forgotten that *we* flow.

We accept our 'station' in life and our identity by the 'class' we were born into, or the uniform we wear, Cleese, Barker and Corbett, the school we went to, the exams we passed and those we failed, the organisation we work for, and the job we do. We accept with unnerving ease the labels that society is willing to throw at us, and if the label sticks and we accept it, so much the better, we have been put in our box and life can resume its natural order.

We assume the identity bestowed on us too easily never really thinking, does the label enable. This has been brought to the fore in recent years after the COVID-19 pandemic. People, rightly or wrongly, depending on which side of the debate you are on, were largely complicit, compliant, conformed, and coerced into staying at home and getting vaccinated. As the workforce was enabled to work from home (WFH), I think when it was safe to return to the office, the traditional place of 'productivity', an existential crisis began to emerge in the general populace, based on the notion that for some, the identity of being part of a workforce in an office was somehow redundant.

Whilst there was never a question, for most people of giving up work, the nature of how, where, and why we went to the office was called into question. An existential crisis was, I think, at the bottom of this. Everything we had assumed, learned, believed, and held up as a place of work could be questioned. Afterall most companies had people, they could trust to be productive; they just didn't necessarily know how to trust them if they couldn't see them.

As Alan Watts (2011) wrote,

> We seldom realize, for example that our most private thoughts and emotions are not actually our own. For we think in terms of languages and images which we did not invent, but which were given to us by our society.

Watts doesn't consider, in this passage, that society may also imbue us with an embedded cognition about how we should feel in relation to certain aspects of our lives, but my sense is that how we should feel, according to outside pressure at any given time, will mainly come at us through the interruption of language.

Perhaps you are starting to think about the cultures that you live, work, and play in, and whether they contribute to your flow or interrupt and dilute it; whether the organisation you work for lets you work unhindered or feels it needs to 'have a handle on what it is you are doing'. You may be considering the academic establishment and the culture that exists there and whether it is trying to truly enable your education or is trying to boost its ratings and therefore attract more funding.

You may question whether it is teaching you what you wish to learn or what it wishes to teach you, or even if it is teaching you the way you learn or the way it wishes to teach you, in the process forgetting the maxim, 'If they cannot learn the way we teach, then perhaps we should teach the way they learn' attributed to Ole Ivar Lovaas, a Norwegian-American psychologist.

There was a recent scandal in British education, as Heads of schools were cheating or encouraging their staff to cheat by enabling students to pass exams so that the school moved up the league table; no one benefits from such a myopic view, especially not the children and society at large. If this trend continues, we will slide towards mediocrity dressed in the emperor's new clothes: Enhanced results from mediocre work. And we can revert to the Strathern quote from earlier, 'when a measure becomes a target, it ceases to be a good measure'.

The subtlety of the things that can block your flow is not to be underestimated. Flow requests that you pay attention to it and in doing so enable your best self to be present in the world, in the eternal now.

If the education system was designed for a specific outcome, that of building compliance to produce widgets, as we have perhaps seen in the Rockefeller example, commerce needs a so-called 'human resource', a somewhat abhorrent term, and fortunately for commerce, humans have a predilection for reproduction, therefore ensuring supply of said resource.

The ties between education and commerce reach back to the days when tradesman needed to subjugate apprentices to learning the trade. The word 'apprentice' has its roots in the Latin 'apprendare' to grasp mentally and then into the old French, 'aprentiz' learner of a trade. By definition, if one is learning a trade, then one is being taught and the teacher sets the curriculum on the basis of the outcomes they need, not necessarily what the apprentice needs to learn for their flow, and like the educational curriculum, the apprentice was tasked with producing a very specific outcome, so that they might, after learning alongside a master craftsman, develop their own style or find their own authentic style. The acclaimed fashion designer, Alexander McQueen, left school with just one qualification and went into apprenticeship in London's famous Savile Row with a tailor of Military uniforms. It obviously served him well and he went on to find his own unique style. I'm not sure it's always the case and I would imagine it is dependent on the field of apprenticeship and what else the apprentice is encouraged to do whilst studying.

I was an apprentice in a different life but was fortunate enough to have someone who taught me early on, what is often attributed to Pablo Picasso, 'Learn the rules like a pro so that you can break them like an artist'. It was a similar phrase adopted by McQueen at his 2015 show, Savage Beauty, at the Victoria and Albert Museum in London.

It is evident that the compliance mindset has been prevalent throughout the industrial revolution and continues to dictate how the business world employs compliance today. For clarity, we are talking about 'compliant' in the sense of, 'consent, accede, yield' for as much as we would tell ourselves that we are in control; we are continually and dangerously yielding the power of our flow, the opposite of what Tennyson talks of in Ulysses, 'To strive, to seek, to find and not to yield'.

Again, we yield because we are complicit in our compliance, for fear of losing the school place, the offer of employment, then employment, and acceptance by our 'superiors', our colleagues our 'society' or 'community'.

I am constantly struck by a seemingly innocuous paradox that we assert our rights to freedom, and thereby flow, and yet we relinquish, all to willingly, our rights to those two pearls, freedom, and flow, through the need to belong and thus comply. It is seemingly a life of compromise and definitely not linear. There are no straight rivers; only water flow is constrained.

How the state build compliance is no secret and has often been brutal and all the major empires, and some of the minor ones, have been guilty of brutality throughout history. Indeed, we see it writ large today as rival religions rape and torture 'non-believers' into leaving 'their' domain. Compliance through terror is acted out on the 21st century stage with common frequency.

But the nation state builds compliance in its citizens through much subtler means. Take an example from 'Hybrid Rule and State Formation: Public-Private Power in the 21st Century' edited by Shelley Hurt and Ronnie Lipschutz (2015), according to which 'Singtel operates the land and mobile phone system as well as the internet. In short, the state can exert considerable influence over much of the information circulating it. By controlling domestic political debates and outcomes, Temasek (the company) is a powerful tool for social control and state building. It has helped mould compliant citizens whose wellbeing is tied to a wide range of government owned firms'.

Then there is a note from Wikileaks, attributed to Bill Ivey in an e-mail to John Podesta, which contains the following, somewhat chilling observation in the run up to the Clinton-Trump election battle, 'And as I've mentioned, we've all been quite content to demean government, drop civics and in general conspire to produce an unaware and compliant citizenry. The unawareness remains strong, but compliance is obviously fading rapidly. This problem demands some serious, serious thinking – and not just poll driven, demographically inspired messaging'.

It is not too hard to imagine an Orwellian type of ministry, say, 'The ministry for flow', which of course in the Orwellian tradition would be the 'Ministry of not flow', whereby a compliant citizenry and by definition, workforce, could be coerced into experiencing 'false flow'. Whilst this might seem farfetched, it's worth considering the way in which hegemony in the telecoms example above is manipulating citizens whose wellbeing is tied to government-owned firms, and that wellbeing is construed in some quarters as an essential component of flow. The process of socialisation is one part of the means through which identity is formed – our sense of who we are.

The second part is in our construing, sense making, the way we form our constructs.

If social psychology is the study of our thoughts, feelings, and actions in relation to others, is it any surprise in a world shrinking at the speed of thought through web2/3, Instagram, LinkedIn, X (formerly Twitter), and Facebook, amongst others, that making meaning of our world, and thereby our worth within in it, becomes harder as our construing is constantly interrupted by the activity of everyone else? It is becoming a fool's errand to try and make meaning through an erratically and rapidly changing world without understanding how we construe it. Thus, Kelly (2003) again suggests, 'both the world in which the person operates and their constructions of it are essential to making sense of them.'

Trevor Butt (2008, pp. 82–83) in his wonderful book on George Kelly, from the Mind Shapers series, wrote,

> Although we may try to separate event from constructions of it, the two are inextricably mixed and cannot be considered separately. We never get in contact with the world 'as it is' – it is always filtered by our constructions of it'.

That said, this is just different to what a 15-year-old would have been experiencing in 1913 on the eve of 'the war to end all wars', or in 1989 when the Berlin wall came down and Francis Fukuyama made his pronouncement about 'the end of history'. The mechanisms of chaos have changed, trying to make sense amidst the chaos has not, we continue trying to understand our place. In Akira Kurosawa's film, 'RAN', a kind of retelling of King Lear, in the aftermath of battle, the King wanders through the ruins and desecration of his land muttering, 'I am lost, I am lost'. Suddenly a jester appears and pronounces, 'Such is the human condition'.

It is the human condition to try and make meaning from our existence, and the idea that flow can enable a more complete existence, if we can embrace it, seems compelling.

The type of education the world needs then, must be a key factor in the teaching of flow, as Julian Astle (2017) states in his article published in the RSA Journal, of which he is the Director of Creative Learning and Development, 'When authoritarianism is the goal, education is the problem. When freedom is the goal, education is the solution'. This thinking may be borne out by the National Education Association (NEA) writing at an annual meeting in 1914,

> We view with alarm the activity of the Carnegie and Rockefeller Foundations – agencies not in any way responsible to the people – in their efforts to control the policies of our state Educational institutions, to fashion after their conception and to standardize our courses of study, and to surround the institutions with conditions which menace true academic freedom and defeat the primary purpose of democracy as heretofore preserved inviolate in our common schools, normal schools and universities.

In the same issue of the RSA journal, Peter Hyman (Issue 3, 2017), in his piece 'Anatomy of learning' writes, 'for an education that is whole we need to develop our sense of discernment, aesthetics, capacity to make music and design products. We need the widest possible opportunities to feel that sense of "flow" made famous by Mihaly Csikszentmihalyi'. The same day this journal landed on my door mat, Phillip Hammond, then chancellor, in his budget announced that secondary schools and sixth form colleges were to get £600 for each additional pupil taking maths or further maths at A-level and core maths at an expected cost of £177 million, as reported on the BBC news website. Could there be a more diametrically opposed vision of what's required than that between Mr Hyman and Mr Hammond?

There seems to be another problem looming on the horizon for education, and whilst the Rockefeller/Carnegie mission seemed to be explicit in manipulating, through the General Education Board, a curriculum that would no doubt serve them, they might have been regarded today by a few as 'venture philanthropists' – a term coined specifically, it would seem, around the technologists in Silicon Valley.

They too claim to be giving something back and in doing so are making available massive amounts of content, search engines that confirm the searchers biases, and accessing for themselves and their investors revenue streams borne out of the user's searches, 'tailored to their needs'. Kirsten Levermore (2017) talks well to this point in her piece, 'The Knowledge monopoly' published in 'Edge' magazine, the journal of the Institute of Leadership (full disclosure, I am a Fellow). She highlights the prevalence of a 'two-tiered educated population, the auto-didactic, information hungry and enthralled searchers, and the passive lazy, "I'll just Google it if I need to" fact finders'.

In the context of flow and how an individual construes it, both these approaches to knowledge acquisition may be valid, but one can't help but wonder what the auto-didactic learns on the journey and what the passive consumer of facts loses. One imagines that the dopamine levels are constantly craving the seek and find instant hit for the passive 'learner', but this is also offset by the fact that dopamine loves 'anticipation' too, so our knowledge-hungry, enthralled searchers may be getting a similar hit.

Steven Kotler and the flow genome project place a lot of emphasis, as we have seen, on the chemicals at play in our brains during 'a flow experience'. However, as the born to flow hypothesis indicates, these chemicals are ever present; indeed we are heavily dependent on them in the fight/flight response.

The flow experience in education is more than the sum total of the chemicals released on our quest for knowledge; however, we come by it. It requires engaged teachers in a valued profession, working in an ecosystem, which is designed to value and appreciate knowledge, and further, the wisdom with which to use that knowledge, to make optimal choices about how we encourage people to evaluate how they will spend three score years and ten interacting with people, their work, and the planet. It requires an understanding that we are born to flow by acknowledging that it is present throughout childhood, in adolescence, and young adulthood. Flow, given the opportunity, will start to shape the way we engage with our future – a future that we create.

To engage with our present and future, we depend on certain structures to 'flow' through our days, weeks, months, and years and some of them come in surprising form and the answer might be less obvious than it seems. Although received wisdom suggests flow only happens when a set of internal criteria are construed and met, having processed some external stimuli, that in itself suggests that our constructs have been created appropriately, nurtured, and fed by community and society at large, which brings to mind the African proverb, 'it takes a village to raise a child'. And within society and community, we are influenced by so many voices that to hear our own call to flow might be difficult, if not at times impossible.

However, we turn again to Butt,

Above all, the person is self-inventing. There is no essential self at the core of the individual, as Rogers and Maslow would have us believe. There is no internal gyroscope guiding us towards our destiny, and we cannot appeal to this make-believe entity to explain away what we have done or not done. The self is an invention, a construction put together by the person in connection with his social world. We are inseparable from our social world, grounded in it just as we are in our physical bodies. Our freedom is 'situated', limited by our bodily and social existence, and we have no access to horizons beyond it. Sartre describes this as existence preceding human essence.

Butt (2008, pp. 82–83) then goes on to cite Sartre, 'He tells us what this means'.

It means that man exists, turns up, appears on the scene, and, only afterwards, defines himself. If man, as the existentialist conceives him, is definable, it is because at first, he is nothing. Only afterwards will he be something, because he himself will have made what he will be' (Sartre, 1995).

We have always been dependent on information, in the form of news, for example, to try and make sense and meaning of the world we live, work, and play in, from the bush telegraph', to unbelievably brave journalists who travel the world in search of the 'truth' and in consuming that news, for that is what one does, we have always been at the mercy of those that would disrupt our flow with their own agenda. This is prevalent in the agenda of the 'cultish' neo-liberalism, as described by George Monbiot, the deliberate manipulation and gaslighting of the populace through ownership of various media channels.

As we enter the era of 'post-truth', 'fake-news', and 'click bate', our will power is lured towards something other than enabling flow to express itself in our lives, and with the insidious manipulation of that wonderful problem-solving tool, the algorithm, any enquiry, however arbitrary, entered into a search engine, which is optimised in favour of the return on investment (ROI) to the stakeholders and owners of the search engine, may well lead you up the garden path and into an echo chamber of their making and your succumbing.

We will talk about church, state, and commerce as well as the way these institutions in the 'wrong' hands can manipulate our meaning making, which in turn can make it harder to reconnect with or enhance our flow. But manipulation of a staple, like the news or information services, makes it harder. Of course, this is not a new problem, but it is a problem that encroaches evermore on the way that we understand liberty and freedom, for example. In the world of post truth and fake news, we are drawn ever deeper into the Orwellian construction, '1984'.

This runs deeper than the way one receives news of the world, and one turns again to the life curriculum foisted upon a complicit and compliant society that eagerly consumes everything with scant regard for its worth, including the news. At the time of writing, when one should be filled with joy at what technology is enabling for the young, just beginning their life's journey into life, one is cognisant of the litany of abuses of power on all sides of the political, technological, and commercial spectra and, as such, the undermining of flow in daily life.

Add to this the account of Rachel Botsman (November 2017), author of *Who Can You Trust? How Technology Brought Us Together – and Why It Could Drive Us Apart* of China's Social Credit System. This system, which will rate the trustworthiness of each of China's 1.3 billion citizens, is being developed by the Chinese Government. The stated purpose of the system is to enhance trust nationwide and build a culture of sincerity. The system is already being piloted on a voluntary basis. By 2022, 80% of the Chinese population is 'enrolled'. Every action of every individual will be monitored and evaluated: What you do with your time, who you meet, what you eat, what you buy on-line, your finances. Everything!

On top of this, your rating will be open to scrutiny by your fellow citizens, your neighbours, friends, and business acquaintances. And you will be ranked against the entire population. This information will then inform your eligibility for a mortgage or a job, where your children go to school. It covers *everything*. The most extraordinary thing about this is that people, in numbers, have already signed up even though it is still voluntary. The Compliant Society, coerced by the state, writ large.

It is axiomatic that a person who recognises their flow and who has the ability to deepen it at will, will make a contribution to a still evolving society far greater than could be imagined by their effort or will only; remember Watts and his view on inspiration, tariki or grace. An example of this may be the 'a-ha' moment or the 'epiphany'; some neuroscientists dispel such an idea and instead postulate that the mind has been working away on the issue at hand for some time and it is only when the student is ready, the teacher, our own mind, appears in front of us with the answer. Somewhere in the background the trickle has turned into a river and the answer flows towards us on it.

If news, education, church, state, and commerce inform our reality and our identity is informed by compliance to societal pressure and the need to constantly please, what chance do we stand against the leviathan force that would lead us to, in the words of Ronnie Corbett's character, 'know our place'?

One could argue that small-town newspapers, back in the day, disrupted flow by reporting on small-town corruption, for example, and that our small-world view was in fact a microcosmic view of the world at large. A counter argument might be that we at least felt connected to something 'real' and therefore our flow in that microcosm, whilst informed by all that is outlined above, at least had some bearing on a direction of our travel. It depends.

If we hold that our 'true north' is something that we inherently know and given Stephen Pinker's assertion that we enter the world with traits and certain dispositions that can be amplified or dampened by our nurturing, then flow might be that 'true north'.

If flow is a factor in our biology, a morphic field, for example, something that underlies our mental activity or perceptions and opens up a new vision, and this is seen as a thing that may well upset the status quo, would a dominant power structure enable more flow in its citizens or workers or would it seek to design a world that demands compliance? Would the power structure be more coercive?

If taken as a conspiracy amongst a ruling elite, this might seem farfetched. However, if the component parts of societies are broken down and have produced a feudal, and strangely similar hierarchical and Westphalian structure support their existence, then perhaps it makes more rational sense.

There is a danger that we stray too far from flow in our search for its inhibitors and enablers and in doing so we muddy the water; this is not my intent. Landing on the notion that we are born to flow demands that we look in some dark corners, as well as at the received wisdom of what flow is and what it isn't.

From the perspective of human performance, it would seem that we have evolved and developed many more inhibitors than enablers, but perhaps this is just how we construe the world. We should, given the marvel of communication technology, be able to enable not only those close to us whom we know well but also those who exist beyond our tribe, community, county, or country. We should be able to empathise with individuals on a journey more readily because technology gives us closer proximity to their experience of living and their excellence in being alive and in flow.

In other words, we should be able to readily understand the many forms of flow that exist not just the canonical version accepted as the 'norm'. But there is a tendency to see the world as we think it is, not as it is, and so we start to believe what suits our own prejudices and biases; as I believe we are born to flow, others will not, and so hence be straying into the realms of life that seem to inhibit or enable flow.

Summary

In this chapter, we see and consider:

- Where attention goes, energy flows.
- If you don't notice that you lack something, you can't improve your performance in that specific area.
- We interrupt another's flow because we have forgotten that *we* flow.
- The subtlety of the things that can block your flow is not to be underestimated.
- 'Learn the rules like a pro so that you can break them like an artist' according to Pablo Picasso.
- We yield because we are complicit in our compliance.
- It is becoming a fool's errand to try and make meaning of an erratically and rapidly changing world without understanding how we construe it.
- 'We never see with the world "as it is", it is always filtered by our constructions of it'.
- Flow, given the opportunity, will start to shape the way we engage with our future.

Exercise/Reflective Practice

1 Reflect on your 'circles of control', a technique for thinking about the right thing. The circles are, 'can't control, can influence, can control'. Draw each circle and at any given point in time when you are struggling with your flow, write in the circles what you can do/can't do/can influence. Knowing intimately the content of the can't control circle will move consciousness towards what you can control and help you move towards more flow. (This is adapted from Dr Ceri Evans' (2019) book, *Perform Under Pressure*.)
2 Reflect on where you are compliant in your life and whether that is driven out of authority, respect or whether you are complicit if it goes against your way of wanting to be in the world.
3 Reflect on your assumptions and whether you are truly cognisant of them and how this shapes your interactions with the world you encounter and by definition, your flowfulness.

4 Consider the subtle things that might interrupt your flow. Are they health, money, comparison with others, the need for acceptance, and the need to own more? Sometimes we are influenced by the ecosystem we inhabit in ways we ignore, often at our peril.

References

Astle, J. (2017). Teaching for freedom. *RSA Journal, 163*(3) (5571), 10–15.

Botsman, R. (2017). *Who can you trust?: How technology brought us together and why it might drive us apart*. Hachette, UK.

Butt, T. (2008). *George Kelly: The psychology of personal constructs*. Bloomsbury Publishing.

Evans, C. (2019). *Perform under pressure*. HarperCollins.

Goleman, D. (1985). *Vital lies, simple truths: The psychology of self-deception*. Simon & Schuster.

Hurt, S., & Lipschutz, R. (Eds.). (2015). *Hybrid rule and state formation: Public-private power in the 21st century*. Routledge.

Hyman, P. (2017). Anatomy of learning. *RSA Journal, 163*(3) (5571), 26–31.

Kelly, G. (2003). *The psychology of personal constructs: Volume one*. Routledge.

Levermore, K. (2017) *Edge Magazine, The Knowledge Monopoly*. 74–75. Institute of Leadership. LID publishing.

McGilchrist, I. (2018). *Ways of attending: How our divided brain constructs the world*. Routledge.

Sartre, J. P. (1995) *Existentialism and Humanism*. 35–36. Methuen

Watts, A. (2011). *The book: On the taboo against knowing who you are*. Vintage.

Chapter 14

The Business of Flow

Channel

Trust is the lubrication that makes it possible for organizations to work.
(Warren Bennis)

Trust in business has its wellspring in flow, and trust should sit at the core of all business endeavours. The more trust that you have in a system, the more flow you will have. However, although cited often as a key component of any business relationship, trust has been diluted through the centuries of nefarious business practices, and consequently both internal and external business relationships have suffered.

From September 2023 to October 2023, the Conservative party in the UK, with Liz Truss at the helm for just 50 days, practically destroyed the UK economy and damaged the trust, both citizens and the markets, had placed in the UK government. Crisis ensued and the calamitous scramble to try and turn the people and the markets was made difficult, if not impossible by the previous PM, Boris Johnson's reputation, compounding the problem. Trust had been lost. Eventually the Conservative party will go on to self-implode, with PM Rishi Sunak announcing a snap general election on 22 May 2024, and the Conservatives losing power to Labour in a landslide victory.

Indeed, the world's population often finds itself at odds with its leadership, both in politics and commerce. One doesn't have to look too far into the past to see how the populace has been duped by business, and as David Ross (2022), author of *Confronting the Storm* writes,

> Leadership is often accused of outrageous behaviour including greed, ego, lack of empathy and exhibitionism. As examples, millions of Wells Fargo Bank's customer accounts were opened fraudulently to boost salespeople's commissions, News Corp editors illegally hacked phones, and Volkswagen (ironically German for, 'people's car'), falsified emissions data on its diesel engines. It is easy to appreciate the adverse ramifications that this has for trust.

And when the global financial crisis emerged through malfeasance and subprime mortgages causing untold misery, the tragedy of Bhopal and the Union

DOI: 10.4324/9781351169929-15

Carbide pesticide plant industrial disaster in 1984, the horsemeat scandal at British supermarket chain Tesco – where in 2013, it was found that 29% of a burger was actually horsemeat and not beef – the tobacco industry, big pharma, and this all originates from bad leadership, flawed practice, a lack of transparency and the demand from the investors for return on investment (ROI) at almost any cost.

In offering a diametrically opposed view to the one that is generally accepted today as truth, that one has to build trust, I would counter with, one cannot win trust; one can only lose it. It is demonstrable that people invariably do not enter into conversations, relationships, and even employment with mistrust front and centre. There is generally a willingness to begin a relationship with some degree of trust in order to build something bigger and better for creating a significant, meaningful future.

If trust sits at the heart of an organisation, flow will be less constrained; people will be more creative, productive, and innovative. There will be clarity of thought and efficiency and effectiveness in the way people find ways through the complexity

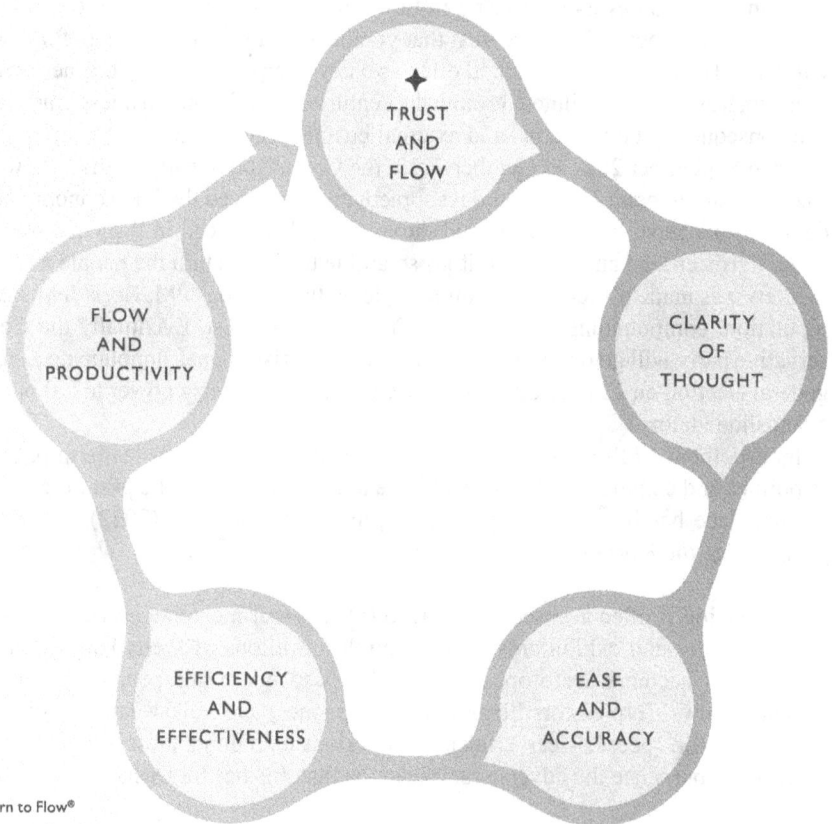

Born to Flow®

Figure 14.1 Flow and trust to flow and productivity

of modern business and a modern world, doing business at the speed of thought. And it is no exaggeration to state, *business at the speed of thought*, given how quickly the markets reacted to the so-called 'fiscal event' announced by Kwazi Kwarteng on 23 September 2022 in the UK, when trust in the Chancellor was paramount. The pound fell against the dollar by 5%, its lowest in 50 years. Reaction was instantaneous.

The trajectory of business and the machinery of efficiency, the tools and instruments that have been developed in response to perceived need for efficiency gains since the industrial revolution, from the Spinning Jenny through to Henry Ford's production line, may have resulted in efficiency and effectiveness, but at a cost, and that cost may be the erosion of trust.

Reducing flow in people ultimately required to drive the business forwards, from the shop floor to the boardroom, has an exponential impact on people's ability to deliver their best selves as the business needs them to. If trust sits at the heart of an organisation, flow will be less constrained; people will be more creative, productive, and innovative. There will be clarity of thought and efficiency and effectiveness (see Figure 14.1)

Performance management systems that forced managers to compare and rank team members against each other, originally intended to improve performance, had sometimes destroyed self-confidence, created rivalries, eroded trust, and damaged flow. People are constrained by the instruments designed to enable their performance or more precisely, productivity i.e., sweat the asset and the primary levers for increasing performance, for example, people, ideas, innovation, curiosity, assets, etc. are ineffective at best and damaging at worst, and yet are often still the levers that leaders reach for.

Summary

In this chapter, we consider, and think about:

- Warren Bennis said, 'Trust is the lubrication that makes it possible for organizations to work'.
- Trust in business has its wellspring in flow, and trust should sit at the core of all business endeavours.
- The more trust that you have in a system, the more flow you will have.
- Indeed, the world's population often finds itself at odds with its leadership, both in politics and commerce.
- 'Leadership is often accused of outrageous behaviour including greed, ego, lack of empathy and exhibitionism' said David Ross.
- One cannot win trust; one can only lose it. It is demonstrable that people invariably do not enter into conversations, relationships and even employment with mistrust front and centre.
- If trust sits at the heart of an organisation, flow will be less constrained; people will be more creative, productive, and innovative.
- Reducing flow in people ultimately required to drive the business forwards, from the shop floor to the boardroom, has an exponential impact on people's ability to deliver their best selves as the business needs them to.

- Performance management systems that compare and rank team members, originally intended to improve performance, had sometimes destroyed self-confidence, created rivalries, eroded trust, and damaged flow.

Exercise/Reflective Practice

1 Think about how trust is emergent in the cultures you live, work, and inhabit.
2 Do you start with trust as you deal in the world of commerce?
3 Do you find that trust is a key component of your flow, both giving trust and being trusted? How do you notice this manifests in your thinking and feeling, and you're feeling about your thinking?
4 If you are ranked according to metrics, KPIs, or through psycho-metric evaluation, does it help or hinder your flow?

Reference

Ross, D. (2022). *Confronting the storm: Regenerating leadership and hope in the age of uncertainty*. Business Expert Press.

Chapter 15

The Flow Leader as Coach

The Potential of Undercurrents

At this point it may be useful to describe how I think about and use flow in my executive and performance coaching practice and how it fits with my philosophy of being born to flow.

Many people work with a coach to enable them to get out of their own way, whether it's project-specific, taking action in context, fear of failing – people are more often afraid of the perceived consequences of failure than the failure itself – or succeeding for that matter, fear of confrontation, handling a given situation or producing a compelling presentation, dealing with imposter syndrome, or just for improving all-round performance. It can be related to any field whether it is business, sport, or life.

There are as many reasons to work with a coach as there are people, and nobody ever hired a coach to get worse at something. So, by definition, the last thing people need is for the coach to get in their way too. Dr Dave Alred is a sports coach who decided to literally get out of the way of the player he was working with; he started to stand alongside them. And people need to get out of their own way to fully enable and own their flow to see and feel potential leaving the body as an improvement in performance, in whatever domain. Two barriers to breakthrough, coach and client, can exist before the coaching even begins.

For a coach to stay out of their client's way during a coaching session and for the client to achieve maximum benefit, it would be ideal for both coach and client to be in flow. This is not as daunting as it may sound. Working on the hypotheses that we are born to flow and that evolution has provided us with all the tools to coach effectively, namely intellect, empathy, and crucially, two ears and one mouth, to quote Epictetus, we should be able to stay out of the coachee's way.

I have spoken about things that inhibit and cause friction in flow and, in a coaching conversation, perhaps the one sure thing that can inhibit the client being in flow is the coach.

If the assumption is that coaching is a conversation during which the emphasis is, 'the art and science of facilitating the learning, development and performance of another' and we trust that the client or player, has within them all of the resource and faculty to deal with the issues, problems, or opportunities (IPOs) they are working on, then perhaps the best way to achieve their desired outcome is to facilitate

DOI: 10.4324/9781351169929-16

them being in flow, and for this to happen, as a coach, your flow intensity should be congruent with that. An undercurrent in the conversation, as the coach can be both leader and follow, as the branching of streams emerge in the conversation.

As a coach, you must be attentive to your flow. Before a session begins, the usual suspects will be present in the shape of flow inhibitors or friction, such as being fully present, have I gotten over the commute or more frequently these days? Is my IT up to the job? Have I left my baggage, assumptions, and anticipations at the door?

You could also consider how you wish to deepen your flow in service of the player deepening theirs and being able to work on their goals with effortless effort, remember the Jonny Wilkinson's interview. Given that we have moved from being dictated to by a prerequisite set of circumstances and conditions being in play to the democratisation of flow, in this book, at exactly the right moment, it is up to you to decide what flow is for you and how you fully associate with it at any given moment, to touch any moment with childlike-ness in a moment of self-forgetful-ness.

For example, if I am thinking or worrying about the next question before I have fully observed my client's thinking or absorbed their answer, the clue is if I'm finishing someone's question in my head, I'm probably not listening attentively. This will inhibit my flow and consequently, my client's. If I am looking for exactly the 'right question' that I think the client wants to hear, I am probably distracted by my own thinking and the need to be 'right' in some way; my flow will be inhibited. And if I'm trying too hard, then brain science dictates that not only does thinking get in the way, but the way that the brain triggers that thinking will inhibit flow.

As a coach, in sport, business, or life, you will know when you have clients in flow and when they could access more. You will recognise from your experience when a session is going well and when there is some tension or friction that inhibits the conversation, and the attention, of the client or your own. After some 25 years of coaching, I am still learning and absorbing 'stuff' into my practice, one example is the powerful statement from McGilchrist (2019), as mentioned previously, in his small folio, *Ways of Attending*, 'Attention may sound a bit boring, but it isn't at all. It is not just another "cognitive function" – it is actually nothing less than the way in which we relate to the world'.

A client in flow is a beautiful thing. The coach trusts the client's ability and resource and probably asks the most basic questions to enable a client to make sense and construct meaning and to harness more of their flow, again the undercurrent at work. For example:

- What would you like to talk about?
- What else might you want to talk about?
- What's most interesting? (opportunity for choice)
- Can you say a *little* more about that? (making them feel safe in not needing to disclose all in one go)
- What would be an excellent outcome for you from this conversation? (assume there is a framework for their excellence, otherwise you can use 'good)

- What else might I need to know to understand this issue/problem/opportunity?
- How would you like this issue/problem/opportunity to change, specifically?
- What options do you have to move this forwards?
- What else could you do?
- If there were no barriers to breakthrough in your performance, what might you experiment with?
- For clarity what are you going to do?
- What's your next deliberate action or area of focus?
- When will you do this?

There will always be context to questions, so please don't be distracted by the example flow above, move on!

In following the client's interest, the coach reduces the amount of flow friction they are introducing into the coaching conversation. This doesn't mean that the questions will not challenge or cause the client to be attentive to their IPOs at a deep level, and of course, the coach needs to complete the mental check list of whether they think the client is comfortable, whether they have rapport, whether they are working on the right topic according to the clients' desired outcomes, etc. By using some questions above, I think that something else happens that enables the clients' flow at a deeper level.

In enabling deeper flow, it is unlikely that we will stimulate the limbic ring or the amygdala in such a way that the emotional response causes flow inhibition through a perceived threat or a fearful reaction to the questions posited above. Of course, the way in which we ask the question, 'What else?', for example, could seem threatening and cause massive emotional response and generate interference, depending on our tone of voice, body language, facial expression, etc.

Whilst this is not a book on neuroscience, in coaching there is a place for considering what happens in the brain in response to certain stimuli and as such, in the context of this book, there is a place for considering what happens to the brain when the coach is accessing and enabling flow, both in themselves and in the client. It is also interesting to note what Antonio Damasio says, 'brain is to biology and mind is to consciousness'.

The proposition of brain science as a way to coach better maybe akin to knowing how the computer in a four-wheel drive can accurately drive each wheel independently in any terrain.

However, if knowing that dopamine, the reward neurotransmitter, works when certain stimuli are introduced, for example, by the number of likes on your Facebook page or a coaching question that generates a person to access their inner resource and find an answer to their IPO then a little brain science must be good.

Acknowledging the neuroscience and the psychological aspects in coaching are ever growing and since it is not the purview of *Born to Flow* to address them in detail, it merely points out that in the ever-changing definition of what coaching will become in the 22nd century, the science will probably have more sway than the 'art'.

Although, in conversation, 9 September 2022, with Professor John Adair, the world's first Professor of Leadership, former UN Chair of Leadership Studies United Nations System Staff College in Turin and responsible for introducing leadership studies to Royal Military Academy Sandhurst he said of Peter Young, his former commanding officer, Arab Legion, that, 'he had a kind of infectious enthusiasm. This chap, he was definitely in flow as far as being commanding officer of a Bedouin regiment, he loved it' and when pressed on how Adair recognised Young as someone in flow he said, 'It was probably his effect on me. Whereas the other lot (officers), didn't do anything for my confidence, etc. There was a kind of creative element that he was drawing the best out of you'.

Encouraging clients to look at their own flow is fairly easy based on the idea that like a river, they are always becoming. And so, like a river, they will ebb and flow, and a person can measure that in whatever way works for them, for example, the intense colour as Laird Hamilton suggests, but more intuitively, how I am feeling, how I am being alive.

For simplicity, there is a somewhat strange, constant need to measure ourselves; it's how we know we are 'winning': Points on the board, runs, try's, touchdowns, speed over distance, sales made, targets reached, waves ridden; but that only tells part of the story. We have seen many times that the scoreboard doesn't reflect what excellence might be to a person who is flowing. And as Eddie Vedder sang in a wonderful song penned by Jerry Hannan, 'Society', 'There's those thinking, more or less, less is more, But if less is more, how are you keeping score?'.

This then seems to be the perennial problem for anyone trapped in a world consumed by the need to gauge their success, outside of their contentment and fulfilment in life.

Can we feel without naming or numbering our flow because that is far more interesting than an arbitrary score that we inherit, as if flow can be measured on some Likert-type scale? To be with feeling your flow, without naming it, is perhaps the greatest challenge as most academicians evaluate flow, post-hoc, using a scale *they* can relate to; so it ticks a box.

But let's say, to begin with, you need a flow compass, a point of reference – it really doesn't matter what you call it, a number, a letter, a colour, a feeling, or some kind of embodied cognition – and suppose you just notice when you wake how you *feel* in your flow, and then you revisit it as you emerge into your day, and you do this in your own way, at your own pace, as you are being, perhaps doing, throughout your emergent day. You are attentive to the waves of flow that wash through you and over you, taking notice of how your flow rises or falls, remembering the integration and alignment of the elements in the model introduced earlier and their interaction will affect your being, as well as what you are doing. The breakthrough might come as a shift in perspective when you suddenly feel different about your own thoughts.

In this environment of paying attention, of noticing, you begin to own your flow and interestingly, I believe, you strengthen your relationship with your self-concept and that enables you to reach further into your endeavours and experimentation with the flow expression of your life. When you grasp this as a coach facilitating the flow and access of your clients to their flowfulness, as an undercurrent, in the moment you are enabling them to construct and access their best selves.

Summary

In this chapter, we consider:

- There are as many reasons to work with a coach as there are people.
- Nobody ever hired a coach to get worse at something.
- People need to get out of their own way to fully enable and own their flow, to see and feel potential leaving the body as an improvement in performance; leaders can help enable this.
- The one sure thing that can inhibit flow is the coach or leader in an organisation.
- 'Attention may sound a bit boring, but it isn't at all. It is not just another "cognitive function" – it is actually nothing less than the way in which we relate to the world'.
- A client, leader, or employee in flow is a beautiful thing.
- As a coach or leader, your presence might be best felt as an undercurrent, gently moving the client or player along, non-directive, just enabling.

Exercise/Reflective Practice

1 Do you recognise, as a leader or coach, when someone is in flow and that it can be beautiful?
2 Consider the idea that as an undercurrent, as a leader you are a facilitator, sometimes leading, sometimes following, but supporting through your flow and challenge.
3 Reflect on your most attentive self, and what ebbs and flows for you as a coach or leader?
4 What disengages you and pulls your attention from the single purpose of the moment, when your presence is an absolute for that, and with that moment, and your leadership needs to fully flow?

Interview: Highlights and Insights from David Hemery, Teacher, Olympian and Author

- To the question, 'is being in flow innate? 'In flow I feel utterly alive, body, mind, emotion, spirit'.
- (In flow) 'being in sync holistically and effortlessly. It isn't a strain to be in flow. In fact, when I was in absolutely super shape in Mexico, it was how much energy I let out into the run. And I was just utterly conscious of the amount of energy needed and the pulling back and the allowing'.

- 'I think (flow) it's to do with alignment, purpose, alignment of your intention. I think that's needed in flow because sometimes if I had been feeling very out of alignment, I just come back onto what's the purpose? what are you trying to do? what contribution are you trying to make? and all of a sudden, the clarity comes, and the flow comes again'.
- 'Self-challenge has always been my motivation since as far back as I can remember'.
- 'I think the intention of humanity, I hope, collectively, is to move towards higher functionality, purpose, vision, mission. Higher functioning in some way and that would be to do with harmony, peace, cooperation and getting better at things and just making it a better world. Nature is phenomenal, it's balanced, it manages to do its thing'.
- 'Mission and purpose are for me the aligning factor. I don't say for everybody, but that's it, for me. It's a really important element of what drives me to do whatever. Particularly making a contribution that's really important. Part of being human and also being me'.
- 'You actually have to have physical energy, to make positive choices to use this. So, the body physical, whether that's through nutrition, enough sleep, whatever, you have to be healthy enough to think positively'.

Reference

McGilchrist, I. (2019) *Ways of attending: How our divided brain constructs the world.* Routledge.

Chapter 16

The Flow through Life
Ebbs and Flows

Thinking about a being in flow inevitably leads to thinking about what interrupts our flow. There are an overwhelming number of things that occur in daily life that, if attended to, will disrupt, and interfere with flow, and it starts very early, as we saw with the child learning to walk. As mentioned, I have called this 'friction'.

In moving through life, the systems that should enable flow are actually not very well designed to facilitate it and examples can be found in the histories and activities of church, state, education, and commerce.

Whether the early school years where the prevalent word is 'no', or senior school where rules are imposed and young minds are melded by the compliant curriculum, which is ultimately designed to produce a compliant workforce. Six Cs start to emerge for us as to what might interfere with being in flow:

- Coerced
- Ccompliant
- Conform
- Complicit
- Collude
- Capitulate

Keep those in mind as you navigate the friction and as you navigate the optimum way to express your flow throughout your life. Another 'C' could be added here that also disables us on the flow journey, complacency, and we become complacent at our peril.

At university, rules and regulations, especially in under-graduate degrees seem, again, to inhibit flow. Instead, our inclination in drifting towards university is eventually to kowtow to a fear-based societal norm. Does one seek an education or a degree; and whilst no one would suggest they are mutually exclusive, they may not be the same thing, as Mark Twain mused, 'I have never let my schooling interfere with my education'. Conor O'shea, former national coach to the Italian rugby team and now director of performance rugby at the England rugby football union (RFU), has a nice turn of phrase when he says, 'sport is an education for life'. Education comes in many guises.

DOI: 10.4324/9781351169929-17

Apprenticeships offer another route into adulthood, and again into a somewhat compliant existence that people neither ask for, nor dream of. It could be reasonably argued that the society that we inhabit and are complicit in perpetuating, is one designed by church, state, and commerce to inhibit flow and thus our boundless abilities towards more fulfilment and better performance. A cautionary note: It is often the systems, structures, and practices that are in place that people will adhere to, sometimes blindly, that can inhibit another's flow.

If church, state, education, and commerce, sound like a clarion call to rail against those institutions that are largely responsible for the shape of society, it is not, and we should explore it a little more, because listening to both sides of a story will convince you that there is more to a story than both sides, as Frank Tyger, the cartoonist and humourist, quipped.

Perhaps an interesting place to start is architecture. At first glance, all three institutions are seemingly enabling flow in the buildings they have created and the instruments that they deploy, looking closer, perhaps all three are manipulating flow within their walls.

Nothing can compare to standing at the entrance to one of the grand awe-inspiring religious buildings. Our attention is generally drawn upwards, stained glass colours our vision, and sound, and lack of it dominates. We are in the presence of master craftsmen, who under instruction have created a space where there is no doubt who is in charge. Our flow is being manipulated through the very architecture that promises so much and yet perhaps delivers so little, except in respect of the adherence to the rituals that take place within it and the constriction of thought. The grand churches, mosques, and synagogues were once the dominant feature on the skyline. They impressed upon the populace that belonging to such an institution would bring you closer to the munificence of heaven.

It could be argued that the great religious buildings have been replaced over the years by the grand architecture of mammon, and whilst the historical significance, ornate façade, and majesty of these buildings cannot be denied, the mighty corporations and banking institutions now dwarf the religious buildings with their fortress like edifice, thereby letting the populace know that there has been a power shift. These monuments to the fiscal are adorned with the supposed trappings of success, the high atrium, representative of the towering ceilings of the cathedrals, the way we are greeted by the uniform identity of the receptionist who will direct us to be seated and we will comply; in the same way we move to be seated in a church perhaps, the way sound circles around us whilst waiting to be ushered into an ante room or whisked half a mile into the sky.

However, the institutional architecture of state has been caught somewhere in the middle, mainly a funding problem, but still fighting for its place on the skyline, as it battles for power and relevance, as church and commerce battle for souls and empires fade. Educational establishments vary globally, as one would imagine, but at a very simple level one would have thought that, as a species, we should be designing collaborative spaces for learning and enabling future generations. In fact, our living legacy should be the work we do today enables those who come tomorrow.

In a world that is subjugated to rules and regulations, to legislation and dogma that claims to enable people, the architecture of church, state, and commerce reflects the same disjunction by inducing awe but stops short of enabling flow. The piece of the puzzle that could push people towards the edge of their own performance, architecture, which could enable flow, is noticeably absent, and instead is used to subjugate.

But all may not be lost; in July 2018, an independent publication placed inside The Times, espoused, 'Future Workplace' and featured articles on 'Why Does Design Really Matter' and 'Importance of Making Work More Meaningful'. Christopher Allen, now Chief Change Officer at Mont Roc Consulting, in his featured piece, 'Why a "Destination Village" is the Future Workplace', says,

> An organisation's culture can be heavily influenced by the appropriate workplace', having previously stated in his piece, 'This evolution can be seen as a grand exercise in trial and error towards developing the future workplace. Each of the iterations (of office workplace design) was designed and developed to improve the way we work, but the quirks of each new development have also highlighted a critical lack of understanding in the way people behave within organisational systems and in their relationship to space.

He goes on to say, 'The rationale is simple: take care of your employees and they will care more, become more engaged and ultimately perform better'. So far so good, but is the design anchored in productivity or in enabling people to fully express their flow? Does design impact their flow, by definition, their well-being and purposeful, meaningful work? The answers seem self-evident.

And Christopher Allen would say 'yes' and at face value he was, and still is, contributing to the wider debate around enabling a workforce. A workforce, that as AI, robotics, the fallout from the global pandemic, and the surge of mass data dictate working lives and careers, will re-orientate at a deeply psychological level, as to how they make a difference to their organisation and to their working lives, as well as their lives in general. And whilst the Hobbesian dictum of the working life of 'nasty, brutish and short' may no longer apply, in the so-called, 'developed' countries at least, existence is in the construing and so is the flow at work.

As the COVID-19 pandemic rearranged the workplace, and continues to cause debate about where people work best or are more productive, there is a question less often asked, where might people flow better in their work and how might we facilitate that?

The 'great resignation' has been talked and written about endlessly, as mentioned earlier, when in actuality we should have been talking about the great existential re-orientation. The sheer mental fortitude that was required to survive and, in some cases, thrive, during the global lockdowns, was demanding in the extreme, and yet mindset was the key all along, adopting a flow mindset could have enabled people and organisations to pace their response. And another question that should have emerged but doesn't seem to have gained prominence, is if the hybrid model is the future of working from home or (WFH), what does excellence look like from that model? Christopher Allen, in June 2024, thinks the hybrid model will gain traction, and perhaps he is right. What is required, as in most things, is alignment and balance.

The 'church' operates at one end of the technological spectrum and commerce at the other, and as David Ross, author of *Confronting the Storm* points out, they both value, in fact depend on hierarchy. In church, we are supposedly isolated from interference and interruption and our thoughts are supposed to be elevated to commune with a higher sense of purpose, to enable us to navigate the complexity of the 21st century with a mindset that emerged 2000 years ago.

Commerce, on the other hand, interrupts continually by using technology to break flow and keep us dangling on the end of a consumerist hook. It continually offers to make our lives better, easier, more meaningful; offers hacks, cheat sheets, and shortcuts, but at the same time, interrupts flow. Choose the multi-platform, metaverse, that at best enables your flow, or better still opt out of the digital morass that plunders your thinking time, and you can increase your flow experience in your life. Life hacks and cheat sheets aren't going to save you; they deprive you of life experience and diminish flow – it's that simple.

However, there may be a link between the entrepreneurial mindset allegedly prevalent in 'millennial's' that is now challenging the status quo by re-imagining the world through products and services like Uber and Airbnb; digital as an enabler of flow.

Jeremy Rifkin, an economic philosopher and architect of the 'third industrial revolution' – a way of thinking about the triple threat of a global economic crisis, climate change, and energy security – in a documentary of the same name, expresses the view that millennials will somehow break the chain of Westphalian thought that has been prevalent for the last 300 years or so: The idea that millennials will flourish to the extent that they are 'buried' in the all-pervasive networks, and this will somehow enable them, and this sits alongside the idea that they are not so dependent on the autonomous agency of the individual; his idea that the pyramid of power will be usurped by the millennial need for joined up, open-source community; and then the development of biosphere consciousness as a way to move through the upcoming disorientation that the world faces as it becomes more VUCA-prone (Volatility, uncertainty, complexity, ambiguity). These are great ideas, but to someone looking to increase their experience of flow, they might seem more akin to life in the matrix than a utopian ideal.

But perhaps, as a millennial entrepreneur, they see a world where their fellow humans feel a pinch or pain point and through their empathy with them, they use technology to challenge the behemoths that have dominated the skyline for so long and it may be, of course, that they are usurping the powers that be singularly for profit.

Perhaps in the technology that people are gradually accepting with their 19th century mindset, they see a flow enabler; they can see a full expression of flow through entrepreneurial empathy in the gig economy. Perhaps technology could be the thing that awakens us from our slumber of existence and propels us into designing and leading a life in flow, instead of one that erects the barriers to breakthrough in performance.

When we examine the workplace or space, do we really find buildings, systems, processes, or architecture that enable flow, or do we once again butt up against the frictions that interrupt our flow expression?

If the entrepreneurs mindset identifies with fellow humans, through an empathetic response to a felt need or pinch pain point, then perhaps the rest of us can fully realise what we are experiencing, for example, an ease in the way we hail a cab, book a holiday, buy a book, or open a new 'bank' account from a fintech challenger bank, for example. A 'bank' that only exists in the cloud and doesn't come loaded with the 18th-century trappings that we have come to expect, i.e. the head office, an outmoded static representation of the brand, and constant bombarding of the populace through never ending media attacks that disrupt our flow, perhaps then we should expect flow as the norm; always on, digitally heightened and enlightened.

Flow is always present and thus if we pay attention to it, we may find that the simple act of attentiveness is enough to increase it. We may find that if we turn practice into perfect practice, we can deepen the existence of flow in our lives further, drawing on the wellspring within. Ultimately if we are attentive to what resonates within us when we notice flow, and we use that flow to enable us to express our lives profoundly, creatively, collaboratively, and competitively, we could find that we achieve a kind of excellence, our peak performance.

I believe that creativity is a flow expression, not that flow is emergent from a creative act. It all starts with recognising that with a trickle of flow, a tsunami can be unleashed, and that we may not be the best in the world but we may find a way to express ourselves as the 'best for the world', to quote Dewitt Jones, National Geographic photographer and film maker, which in and of itself is a kind of peak performance, although Susan Jackson et al. in their 2001 paper described peak performance as a standard of accomplishment.

This is an interesting distinction and clarification, as it was when Maro Itoje suggested there was a difference between high performance, which he thought was personal and subjective, and elite performance, when he appeared on The High Performance Podcast and clarified his distinction with the following, 'I think elite performance is performing at the very top level in your given field', which seemed to cause both Jake Humphrey and Professor Damian Hughes, the hosts, to reflect on his construing as it was the first time in 176 episodes of that podcast that someone had made a distinction.

For clarity, I am not declaring that all people can be great at all things all of the time; I am expressing an axiomatic belief that flow is within us all of the time and attentiveness to it leads to a fulfilling existence and can, in turn, lead to breaking free of receiving knowledge or wisdom unquestioningly. The intent of my writing is to enable different thinking about flow, to gently and perhaps not so gently challenge, to evoke and provoke a different train of thought, a different discourse.

The born to flow hypothesis, I believe, is a moving one, that whilst we are not all born the same, we are born equal, in the context of the subject under discussion, and within that the ability to determine, should we choose, to live with 'our' flow, is something to perhaps be remembered, nurtured, taught, and orientated towards.

I also hold another hypothesis in relation to flow, that the natural state is for humans to commune. So our strongest, most potent selves can manifest when we exist in the close proximity of others and, if this is true, then why have I decried that hypothesis in my condemnation of church, state, commerce, or community in relation to flow, for example?

There is a difference between societal pressure and community demands levelled at an individual, as opposed to, say, a community or society enabling heightened existence through communing with someone to share deep thoughts or feelings – whether you share that with a group or another individual. As a Yale University psychologist, Laurie Santos suggests in a 2019 interview, 'all the studies suggest happiness isn't about self-care. It's about being open to others and being other-oriented in your experiences'.

But I observe something puzzling in relation to my construing of flow and it's this: As a 'community' emerges from the collective need or want of a group of like-minded people, something seems to happen in tandem – an arrangement of hierarchy begins whilst members of the community position themselves into some semblance of belonging. Sir John Whitmore (2003, pp. 148–151) observed this in his book, *Coaching for Performance* through his IAC model – inclusion, assertion, co-operation – for teams, and he writes,

> one macrocosmic example to challenge your mind is the suggestion that the whole of western industrial society is in the latter days of the ASSERTION stage with a few early signs of CO-OPERATION showing through (concern for the environment: the development of European integration). The collapse of the Soviet Empire was the inevitable result of the attempt to coerce that society into the COOPERATION stage without allowing organic development through the previous stages. And the attempts to redraw the map in eastern Europe and elsewhere are a manifestation of a temporary backslide into INCLUSION issues. For some, even SURVIVAL and SAFETY are foreground.

In addition, M. Scott-Peck (1987, pp. 86–103) built his model around 'pseudo community, emptiness, chaos, community', and invariably we must mention Tuckman's 'forming, storming, norming, performing' model. All of these, and there are plenty more, perhaps point us in the direction of how teams and communities form, and within which we can detect how 'leaders' emerge in that landscape.

And, along with leadership comes privilege, and I don't mean the privilege of leading to serve, but the privilege of status, of rank and station amongst the group, team, or community. The cracks may begin to appear around an imbalance, as inclusion gives way to assertion, the two things that Whitmore says must happen before the group or team, and perhaps community, can truly cooperate or collaborate.

It could be suggested that 'community' has somewhat become a modern malaise; that it has become a social heuristic, especially when used by those who would have us gather around a cause, or come to that, the way in which we are encouraged to engage with tech. You can't have a relationship with tech; by definition a relationship is two-way and tech is completely agnostic. Facebook has created a 'global community' of just over three billion monthly users, and within that, smaller communities where people can gather, albeit virtually, without the inconvenience of actually getting to know someone in person, it also create an echo chamber effect.

Influencers influence their followers by inviting them to join in the 'pseudo' community; these are not communities in the sense we have come to know them, they are changing the way we engage with each other, moving us from the deep privilege of sharing a space and place in time to a place where the ephemeral counts as a connection. It may be that we have developed in such a way that it is acceptable for us to engage with our communities, and with society, in such a way, but to do so is to miss one of the very things that enable us to flow – the ability to commune.

It is this point that Jeremy Rifkind in the third Industrial revolution is optimistic about, that millennials buried in the sharing economy and the networks are somehow more engaged than 'other', and that they care more and are somehow more attuned to what is emerging in the environment. For my part I grew up when the milkman used an electric cart or horse to deliver milk, in recyclable bottles, and when returning a soda bottle to a store brought a financial reward; that reward may just have been cost saving, but it was part of an economy that was circular, and the community understood it and was fairly well embedded in it and it was quite low tech.

If then, we are to commune with others, we must be able to commune with ourselves – a deep and meaningful honesty in where we come from, where we are going, how we are getting there, and how we flow through and with our communities.

In being pressed on levels of flow, I have expressed the idea that 'To flow is to commune with oneself and to begin to express one's potential in such a way that the whole of oneself understands it'. It feels like a feeling thing to me, a 'being' thing not a 'doing' thing. The doing emerges out of the flow being, in much the same way I believe that creativity is a flow expression, and not necessarily emergent from the creative act. I know one could argue chicken and egg, but I think flow is the egg from which the act emerges.

If a better performance is more of our potential flowing from the body, at a level we have experienced only fleetingly and infrequently, then we can work *within* ourselves to improve our knowing and understanding and flowing out in the world. This can, of course, be to steady the internal self amid any maelstrom that may beset us; anything that may disrupt our flow requires our participation in it, whether that is grieving for a loved one, toxic behaviour in the workplace, or the disruption caused by any team, group, or community, however construed, that no longer enables us and our flow.

Our sense of just how much a community can contribute to our wellbeing and how much we may give to and serve our communities is summed up well by George Bernard Shaw, and whilst I admit to being fully biased in my interpretation of Shaw's (1903) words, they seem to have an axiomatic relationship to flow,

> This is the true joy in life, being used for a purpose recognized by yourself as a mighty one. Being a force of nature instead of a feverish, selfish little clod of ailments and grievances, complaining that the world will not devote itself to making you happy.

And then

> I am of the opinion that my life belongs to the whole community and as long as I live, it is my privilege to do for it what I can. I want to be thoroughly used up when I die, for the harder I work, the more I live. I rejoice in life for its own sake. Life is no brief candle to me. It is a sort of splendid torch which I have got hold of for the moment and I want to make it burn as brightly as possible before handing it on to future generations.
>
> (Henderson, 1918)

'I rejoice in life for its own sake'. I wonder what happens if I rejoice in my latent flow for its own sake, if I give myself to it fully, let it flow through me so that I meet my better self, if I recognise my flow as an enabler of that mighty purpose?

For clarity, the first extract above is from *Man and Superman*, written in 1903 and the second comes from one of his characters' speeches, and can be found in *George Bernard Shaw: His Life and His Works* by Archibald Henderson. But these two extracts are separate; they were never conceived as a single paragraph, but the world of the web has erroneously thrown them together, as if they were one thought written by Shaw. Still, it doesn't diminish the power of what he is saying.

Summary

In this chapter, we see, encounter, and consider:

- The corollary of thinking about a being in flow inevitably leads to thinking about what stops us being in flow.
- There are an overwhelming number of things that occur in life that, *if* attended to, will disrupt and interfere with flow.
- Systems that could enable flow are not very well designed to facilitate it.
- Six Cs start to emerge that interfere with being in flow: Coerced, compliant, conform, complicit, capitulate, and collude.
- Another 'C' disables us on the flow journey: Complacent or complacency.

- In a world that is subjugated to rules and regulations, to legislation and dogma that claims to enable people, the architecture of church, state, and commerce reflects the same disjunction by inducing awe but stops short of enabling flow.
- After COVID-19, we should have been talking about the great existential re-orientation around what work is, and what it is for.
- Millennial entrepreneurs see a world where people feel a pinch or pain point and through their empathy with them, they use technology to challenge the behemoths that have dominated the skyline for so long or they are usurping the powers that be singularly for profit.

Exercise/Reflective Practice

1 As you reflect on your flow in and, through your life, what frictions cause your flow to ebb?
2 How can you curate a life that resists the interruptions of things that you could avoid being attentive to if you weren't buying into a system? For example, could you curate a life where technology serves you rather than you serving it?
3 When you are looking for a space, place, and time to be creative or optimally productive, what criteria do you select and further, do you know what optimum productivity is for you?
4 When you consider the six Cs we have identified as being detrimental to the complex, dynamic, psychological process of your flow: Coerced, compliant, conform, complicit, capitulate, and collude, do you know in what specific aspects of your life these may be impeding you? For example, are you sometimes coerced into doing certain tasks at work? Do you find yourself conforming to try and fit in, even though it makes you uneasy? Have you ever been complicit in the way that rules have been bent to suit the needs of an organisation? There are many aspects of your flow-life that are dominated by the six Cs if you become complacent.
5 As you reflect on how and where you do your best work, do you understand the great enablers in your work life with regard to your creativity or productivity?

'Interview Insights and Highlights': Conor O'Shea, Director of Performance Rugby, England Rugby

(The emphasis for Conor, when we spoke, was on how flow related to his leadership and the team.)

- 'We've talked about flow being, in my vernacular, momentum. So, if you encourage people to develop momentum, you're going to increase your productivity as long as you're doing the right thing'.
- (On the conceptualisation of flow and what are we really talking about and labels) 'How many different phrases are there for flow? In the zone? Mental toughness?'

- 'Johnny Miller was the heir to Jack Nicklaus. He was blond haired, golden child. Nicklaus was in his 30s Johnny Miller came up the ranks, won the USL open, he won the PGA. Won the British Open, was incredible. I think he's won three of the four major not all four was young, good luck in taking over from Nicklaus documentary was about how he lost it. How he lost the invincibility. And he described the moment that he played his absolute best going down the stretch with Trevino, Nicklaus, Watson and him, so three of the greatest golfers of all time, and he played his absolute best, and the last time he came off, going, "my best isn't good enough". And he said, his description, was every team, every sports person has the moment where they lose that invincibility cloak, that we all have. And I suppose is the reason why I think about flow in that respect, I'm always looking at how you get it back when you lose it. Because I think that's what marks you out, how do you get out of the zone, but get yourself back into it. That's what I'm all about'.
- 'I think in every match that we play in, in every environment, doesn't matter if it's business or whatever, you have, if you can't live the bad moments and come out the other side your stuffed'.
- 'So, my search, and that's what drives my mind, is the mentality of actually getting yourself back on task'.
- 'How can you get people to understand that the (single') "moment" doesn't derail everything, and that's what marks good sports people apart?
- 'The concept of flow. I know what it's like on the golf course, I'm in the zone, and I had to lose it as well. And I'm on the putting green. And that's a starting point for me, it's great'.
- 'I always talk about little moments. And the work we do is about making little moments go your way and matches, these little moments can make big momentum swings'. (Conor uses momentum as a way of describing flow in our conversation context.)
- 'The momentum of the match that we gave away, one moment of not doing your job can change the mentality'.
- (When coaching Italy, 2016–2019) 'The brain of the opposition is always relaxed. (they're thinking) I'm going to my golf course and I'm playing the par four, i.e. Italy. It's easy, birdied it millions of times. I'm not playing the par five that's got narrow fairways, it rough all over the place, the water. We were constantly playing teams who were liberated mentally. So, they have a natural flow that we don't have. But what we can do is we can change that flow during the game by what we do'.
- (On flow interruption) 'There's no-one hasn't got baggage. (and there's) No one who doesn't know how to learn how to deal with baggage'.
- (On team flow and collaboration). 'Giving flow to a team is giving them a belief or giving them an energy and giving them a confidence, giving them an ability to believe in themselves'.
- 'I think sports gives you an education for your life. And it gives you an education for understanding what it's like to battle through exams, and how to have

bad exams and come back and have good exams. Understand that you might not be good at every subject, you mightn't be good at every sport. And I think we let our children down by the pressure we're putting on them'.

- (On what coaching kids for flow could be) 'I think we coach kids to win, as opposed to fulfil their potential. I think we put guidelines on what they are, what they're supposed to do, we inhibit them in terms of how they play'.
- (On building teams and confidence) 'So rather than focus on what we don't have, let's look at what we have. Let's maximise that, and then build on that, as opposed to focus on the negatives, which will get inside people's heads. So do what we do well, focus on what we do well, and then in the background, we work on all the things that we need to make it better, which allows a better flow'.
- (On whether flow could be additive) 'My job as a leader, I think, is to make sure that I maximise the potential of every single person in my organisation. If I'm allowed, to make you the best physio, you can be making the best biomechanics, you can be the best nutritionist, the best prop. So, I should be encouraging them to flow, if I can'.

References

Henderson, A. (1918). *George Bernard Shaw: His life and works, a critical biography (authorized)*. Boni and Liveright.

Jackson, S. A., Thomas, P. R., Marsh, H. W., & Smethurst, C. J. (2001). Relationships between flow, self-concept, psychological skills, and performance. *Journal of Applied Sport Psychology*, *13*(2), 129–153.

Scott-Peck, M. S. (1987). *The different drum; Community making and peace*. Simon & Schuster.

Shaw, B. (1903). *Man and superman: A comedy and a philosophy*. Binker North.

Whitmore, J. (2003). *Coaching for performance: GROWing people, performance and purpose*. Nicholas Brealey.

Chapter 17

The Nature of Flow

Tributary

If flow is a name for something, for a complex, dynamic, psychological process, as I believe it is, or mind-shift or a way of experiencing moments in time if not your lifetime, perhaps expressing oneself, then it also names what flow is not. As such, flow is a construct and is only real in the mind and experience of the construer, and whilst pre-requisite conditions for flow may exist, if flow is thought of too narrowly, then it may become unattainable and somewhat esoteric for 'ordinary' people, whatever that means. Flow is not a measurement of the individual human experience. Perhaps flow lives in the mind, a non-physical part of our make-up, but expresses through the brain and body, the physical part. If we measure the brain and body, are we really measuring flow? My guess, at this stage of our technological evolution is, no.

As soon as we name something, we also name what it is not, and who are we to say how or what another person is experiencing is or is not flow. Flow so far seems to be predicated on a task at hand, skillset available, and challenge of the task, and once immersed in that task, a 'feeling/experience' of flow emerges. An experience and output of peak or optimal performance is the result, and one then returns to 'an ordinary' state; however, that is construed or thought about, and just the thinking could be the constraint. But something else is at play, perhaps.

What if 'flow' calls an athlete to challenge themselves from deep within, an artist to paint and express their inner vision, a musician to compose, a writer to write, a teacher to teach and, their flow is inextricably linked to 'their purpose' and the experience of flow, once it is linked to purpose or being, enables peak performance or optimal experience?

Perhaps an intensity scale for flow would work, or as Laird Hamilton suggests, 'I would imagine it (flow) to have a big spectrum, and that there would be all different colours of flow, like a rainbow', and for a man who spends his time on the very edge of existence and emergence, who are we to say whether he flows or not?

If because of circumstances, we are not engaged in fulfilling our purpose, but engaged in the act of living and being, does that mean that flow will not or should not be available to us? Csikszentmihalyi doesn't think so, and describes how people engaged in 'just doing' everyday jobs 'learn' to enjoy them in a way that is

DOI: 10.4324/9781351169929-18

facilitated by being in flow. *Born to Flow* suggests that 'life' is a flow endeavour and as Joseph Campbell offered, 'to live the ordinary life in an extra-ordinary way'.

Perhaps we do not enter the flow state, it is present, and that latent flow enables us, if we are attentive, waiting for the rush of the tide, and as we discover our potential, our passion, our intrinsic motivation, we turn the tap a little and the flow experience, that of flow flowing through life, enables peak performance and deep psychological experience. The art and act of a being in motion are enabled fully through our subjective flow experience. We have control.

We should consider flow as simply an experience or is somewhat more involved than, perhaps as posited here, a dynamic, complex, psychological process. What if flow, as a composite part of our existence, has been carried through the eons of time; flow as part of our biology, for example? Maybe it makes sense to think of flow in these terms. I think it enables the humble human beings from any walk of life to access flow more easily if construed this way. I think it adds value to simply consider it, and then understand your own flow, as it exists and moves you.

Let us suppose that 37 trillion cells, pulsing in your body right now, have inherited the ability to be constantly in flow, carrying the legacy of your ancestors. And we know life's primary function is to procreate, but on our way, we find or construe its meaning and purpose, and the capability to unlock the meaning and purpose is revealed through flow. Then, perhaps it's more accessible as a way of interacting with the process of living. It becomes more solid for us as part of our make-up, our DNA, and we know, through the human genome project that although we understand about 92%, geneticists don't fully understand it.

It seems that there are some constants in construing flow as an act of achieving a 'different' state that sit outside the current flow orthodoxy, and those constants seem to be linked closely to the nature of our being. Homeostasis is our body in flow. We breathe in and then out; under exertion, breathing happens at a faster rate ensuring oxygen supply to our blood, which enriches the muscles, and so on. Flow has emerged in breathing, optimally.

When flow is stymied by any disease or atrophy, stagnation sets in resulting in death: No flow. So perhaps 'dead' is the word for 'no flow'. As an exercise, try to think about breathing, breathing in and out. Do it continuously and see how long you last. Flow takes care of it for you because it's innate.

Ancestry, the nature of our stories, in a place and time may enable us to flow easily through life if we are comfortable in our 'own skin' and have a solid self-concept. We may be at ease with our personal history, culture, myth, and flowing. If we are uncomfortable with, or out of alignment in some way with the moment we are in, or our own personal myth, flow may become like a spring tide pool, knowing the incoming tide is on its way and will reinvigorate the ecosystem that the flow may have become moribund in. But it is within our gift to know and return to the source through the incoming tide.

If we are cognisant that flow is present and emergent in our living history, our ancestry, and our direction of travel, whether we conceive or construe it to be so or not, we have a better chance of understanding what it is for our own personal relationship with flow. It depends!

Summary

In this chapter, we think about, consider, and see:

- Flow is a complex, dynamic, psychological process. As such, flow is a construct and is only real in the mind and experience of the construer.
- Flow is not a measurement of the individual human experience. Perhaps flow lives in the mind, a non-physical part of our make-up, but expresses through the brain and body, the physical part.
- If we measure the brain and body, are we really measuring flow? My guess, at this stage of our technological evolution is, no.
- I suggest 'flow' calls from deep within and is answered through physical expression.
- We can flow without fulfilling our purpose, engaged in the act of living and being.
- Csikszentmihalyi describes how people engaged in 'just doing' everyday jobs 'learn' to enjoy them in a way that is facilitated by being in flow.
- To flow is 'to live the ordinary life in an extra-ordinary way'.
- The art and act of a being in motion are enabled fully through our subjective flow experience. We have control.
- What if flow, as a composite part of our existence, has been carried through the eons of time; flow as part of our biology, for example?
- We can find or construe meaning and purpose of life, and have the capability to unlock the meaning and purpose through flow. Then perhaps it's more accessible as a way of interacting with the process of living.
- Through the human genome project, we understand about 92%, but geneticists don't fully understand our DNA.
- When flow is stymied by any disease or atrophy, stagnation sets in resulting in death: No flow. So perhaps 'dead' is the word for 'no flow'.
- It is within our gift to know and return to the source of flow, through the incoming tide of life's quest for life.
- If we are cognisant that flow is present and emergent in our living history, we have a better chance of understanding what it is for our own personal relationship with flow.

Exercise/Reflective Practice

1 You are no doubt aware of when your mental state changes – the shift from calm to agitated or from happy to sad, for example – and no doubt, you can pay attention to these changes in state. But by definition, you are not agitated all the time, you are not sad all the time (all things being equal, of course). My guess is

that you notice these changes in state or someone else notices them for you and points it out. Is there a reason that you don't notice flow as a change in state and if you do, what, specifically do you notice?

2 What could you 'measure' to understand your flow at a deeper level? (Don't be constrained in your thinking or feeling your way to this.)

Interview Highlights and Insights from Laird Hamilton, Big Wave Surfer, Entrepreneur, Author, Innovator

- (In flow) 'I think that when things are optimum, thinking is probably too slow'.
- 'Well, flow from me is ultimately the nature of water, that flow really is the movement of water, flow is the characteristic or the way in which water moves, the way it is always in continuing movement. And it is always searching for the path of least resistance'.
- (Flow) 'It's when you're not in your own way. When you become part of whatever it is you're doing, whether you're in the ocean you become part of the ocean, if you're a wave you become part of the wave, you know you're in the wind you become part of the wind, you're on the mountain you become part of the mountain, you become part of the activity you are doing, but not the activity itself, but where you are doing the activity'.
- 'For me I feel when I have my best moments, I'm outside of myself and I'm just acting in a real unconscious way, something that I'm not participating in, which is like when a baby accomplishes flow without trying to accomplish flow, you know, like water isn't trying to accomplish flowing, it just flows and if it's not flowing it looks for another place to flow'.
- 'What your levels are, in whatever discipline you're doing, there's always a moment of thinking and not thinking and then depending on your skill or should I say depending on your experience, the volume of your experience, the non-thinking part is more dominant, and the thinking part becomes less and less and less as you are able to refine the technique and make it more part of your unconscious'.
- 'There's purpose to my life, that I'm doing something, or I've done something that I was meant to do, that I was meant to act in this state of unconsciousness, and I get a sense of fulfilment from doing that and being in that flow state and I get a feeling of accomplishment, of exhilaration, of purpose, of worthiness, of just that there's meaning'.

Part II

Flow

The Devotion to Potential:
It's a Campaign

Do I contradict myself?
Very well then, I contradict myself,
(I am large, I contain multitudes.)
(Walt Whitman, Song of Myself, 51)

Chapter 18

Branching Streams Flow in the Darkness

Tributary: A Dedication to Shunryu Suzuki

I will précis this part of the book by explaining a 'flow' that I worked out on my journey towards understanding that we are born to flow.

So, there is no misconstruing; I want you, as the reader, to understand something that has been in my mind for the last 50 years give or take; I don't believe in accidents, and I don't believe in luck and it's important to understand why. Both words, luck and accident, are ancient and have lost their original meaning; they have become an attribution, a laziness if you like.

We can, and often do, attribute another's success to luck without really considering either what we mean, or what the word really means, or what they did to get lucky. Often, it's the phrase attributed to Gary Player, the golfer, 'the harder I practice the luckier I get' and Serena Williams offers, 'Luck has nothing to do with it, because I have spent many, many hours, countless hours, on the court working for my one moment in time, not knowing when it would come'. So maybe there is a lesson there for those practising and developing their own flow expression; consistency, persistency, mastery, techniques, and tools to embed flow, like tennis, in their lives.

The same applies to 'accident' which simply means, according to its etymology, to 'happen' or 'to fall'. Once again, the word is used without consideration for what we actually mean or where the word originated (Chambers, 2002). It's a shortcut and a kind of heuristic to explain something away.

When I spoke with Professor Tom Treasure, cardiothoracic surgeon and Honorary Professor in the Clinical Operational Research Unit at UCL, he talked about the erosion of language or the way in which it becomes trivialised and, sometimes by necessity, it has to be rebranded because assumptions about the words used take away from the original meaning. He said,

> I think there's undoubtedly times when the same thing gets rebranded for good reasons, partly because the previous word has become trivialised. So, we, (Medical profession UK) for example, when we started formally saying we need to measure quality of life, and people would say, 'Yes, it's all about quality of life', and making it far too simple and notwithstanding, that it isn't a trivial matter, it's actually a matter of actual formula. So, the people who work in that now call it PRO's, patient reported outcomes, but it's a way of rebranding.

DOI: 10.4324/9781351169929-20

Here's my flow is in relation to born to flow; within time, there is a timing. Within timing, there is a chance. Within chance, there is an opportunity for an outcome, either positive or negative, and if you delve into the etymology of luck, accident, and chance, you will find linkages. However, what chance gives us is the opportunity for the dice to land on the right number. We are the agent throwing the dice and there is chance, which has a strange etymology, that something takes place, especially unexpectedly, the falling of the dice, for example. But language has excluded the thrower.

Back to the flow, within time, there is a timing. Within timing, there is a chance. Within chance, there is an opportunity for an outcome, either positive or negative. So to increase our opportunity of optimal outcomes or success, we should seek to put ourselves in the 'place of most potential' as often as possible. Remember, success leaves clues and Williams reminds us, 'luck has nothing to do with it'.

Nathan Burgh writes about the novelist Neil Gaiman's three-step process for putting himself in the place of most potential, although he doesn't call it that. Burgh writes that

Gaiman 'shares the three constraints he uses when writing or creating, Tools, Space and Activity'.

Under tools, Burgh, writes, 'The tools you use dictate your creative output'. He quotes Gaiman,

If you're writing on a computer, you'll think of the sort of thing that you mean and then write that down and look at it and then fiddle with it and get it to be the thing that you mean. If you're writing in fountain pen, if you do that, you wind up with a page covered with crossings out, so it's actually much easier to just think a little bit more. You slow up a bit, but you're thinking the sentence through to the end, and then you start writing.

Burgh concludes that, 'Computers let your writing balloon. Your story loses its shape and focus. But writing with a pen forces you to consider every word, every sentence, before writing. Your story stays sharp'.

Then Burgh turns to space and its use,

Ian Fleming wrote James Bond in two weeks. *Excuse me?!* Ian booked rooms at the crappiest hotels in the most boring towns he could find. Then he stayed there until his book was finished. Basically, he gave himself a crazy incentive (get back to normal life) to get the job done. Neil adapts the idea to his own writing. But instead of going to the crappiest spots, he prefers the quietness of the beach.

Burgh builds on this, 'The key is eliminating distractions in your environment'

• No phone

- No other tabs open
- Definitely no Twitter

He then moves on to activity citing Gaiman again,

When sitting down to work, Neil gives himself two options:

1 Do nothing
2 Write

Neil can sit and do nothing. Just stare into space. Or write. After a few minutes, writing becomes a lot more appealing than doing nothing.

Burgh warms to his subject,

Neil controls his external environment, the tools available to him and the space he occupies, while also limiting his own possible activities within that environment. The three constraints:

1 Where you are
2 What tools you have
3 What activities you allow yourself

If you think of it like a four-sided yard, you now have three fences. Leaving you only one direction to travel. The right constraints incentivize focus, creativity and, as a result, better stories.

Burgh published his thoughts on Medium, an online venue that describes itself as, 'a place to read, write and deepen your understanding'

I think this is a wonderful example by Burgh and we can apply it to increasing our flow when most of the distractions we open ourselves up to can impede it.

And we can close on Voltaire who said, 'Play the hand you are dealt like it was the hand you wanted'.

Summary

In this chapter, we consider:

- My suggestion, following on from Whitman's stanza in 'Song of Myself, 51', 'Do I contradict myself? Very well then, I contradict myself (I am large, I contain multitudes.)', you are allowed to change your mind, contradict yourself, and go on adventures. It is the beauty, nature, and complexity of what it is to adventure as a human being.

- Both words, luck and accident, are ancient and have lost their original meaning, they have become an attribution, a laziness – a social heuristic or explanatory principle.
- We can, and do, attribute another's success to luck without really considering what we mean.
- Gary Player, the golfer, said, 'the harder I practice the luckier I get' and Serena Williams offers, 'Luck has nothing to do with it'.
- There is a lesson for those practising and developing their own flow expression; clarity, simplicity, consistency, constancy, persistency, mastery, meaningful, significant effort, actions, and letting go.
- Professor Tom Treasure talks about the erosion of language and the way in which it becomes trivialised, Language satiation, and, sometimes by necessity, a thing or procedure has to be rebranded because assumptions about the words used take away from the original meaning.
- Within time, there is a timing. Within timing, there is a chance. Within chance, there is an opportunity for an outcome, either positive or negative. So to increase our opportunity of optimal outcomes or success, we should seek to put ourselves in the 'place of most potential' as often as possible, remembering success leaves clues.
- You can use the power of constraints to put yourself in the place of most potential, for example, switch off your phone to have meaningful family time. This might also be discipline.
- You can use friction to drive creativity. In the same way, Michael Jordon used friction to drive his game mindset. Gaiman used friction of boredom to drive him to action, and Fleming used miserable accommodation.
- Voltaire said, 'Play the hand you are dealt like it was the hand you wanted'.

Exercise/Reflective Practice

1 In relation to your flow, specifically, and perhaps in life generally, consider the language you use, its power, or implication.
2 Refine your language as an enabler of mind-shift, for example, does the label enable?
3 What enables you to refine and use language so that you develop awareness of your flow and your evolution as a being in flow?
4 How do you curate space, place, and time to reflect, develop, and evolve?

Reference

Chambers, A. (2002). *The chambers dictionary*. Allied Publishers.

Chapter 19

Engaging with and Owning Your Flow

Tributary

The notion 'Born to Flow' should have led you to conclude, that how you define, refine, and engage with your flow is within your gift. As we delve into Part II, I will share thinking on how you can bond with your flow through alignment, integration, and connecting with yourself and the ecosystem you live in. If we are to integrate, we must align, and what we are aligning to are the differentiated, but overlapping elements within our sphere of influence and concern, as laid out in Figure 5.1.

These pages are not a 'how to' guide. I merely share with you tools, techniques, experiments, exercises, and thinking and suggest that our attentiveness to our flow journey has led me to find these things of use.

I would encourage you, based on your sense making of flow and how it fits with your life and your engagement with it, to build out your experiments and your thinking. You would have, hopefully, already explored, through some of the reflection practices and perhaps tuned into some of the interviewees' take on flow and found things that resonate and propel you forwards in your exploration.

The journey to developing the born to flow hypothesis and then building it out and advancing it further, has its roots in some very specific areas of my life: Illness and severe injury, martial arts, I am not an expert but have enjoyed the discipline, camaraderie, and sometimes community, and wisdom of different styles, teachers, and students, time in the ocean and being in, on, and around water generally. My study of George Kelly and John Boyd and, of course in my professional life as an executive and performance coach, where I have been fortunate enough to study and work with two of the innovators of executive coaching in the UK and Europe, and whose reach has spanned the globe, the late Sir John Whitmore and the very much alive, Myles Downey, founders of Performance Consultants and The School of Coaching, respectively. However, being a father and a husband is top of the list for the sheer pleasure of watching, with my wife, my daughter grow and flow.

To reiterate on some of the critical tributaries to engaging with, and enhancing your flow, you will recall that I have identified that it has centred around the axiomatic idea that it is a part of our being: A dynamic, complex, psychological process, not a state to enter. If you can construe that flow is part of your existence and that you are born to flow, then it might be useful to work out ways that this could

DOI: 10.4324/9781351169929-21

be useful in real terms. To recap, there are key steps to making this work for you and they revolve around the following:

Remembering: You have experienced flow and forget it because there was no need to encode it for retrieval. These memories are likely to be from your childhood, given its over representation in our memory. As the conductor, Charles Hazlewood recalled, 'So, when I was young, I found all that flow. And then only to have it kind of, completely drummed out of me with my first bloody and bruising encounters with the professional business'.

Recognising and retrieval: The power of emotional connection to your flow experience is important. You can fully associate with some aspect of flow and you can reproduce it in your life today or at least vividly recall and retrieve and apply pragmatically.

Reconnecting: This involves bonding with flow through full association, if possible, and awareness of its companionship throughout your life, construing flow in your own way. Identity, society, and community all have their part in our relationship with our flow. The ecosystem we dwell in also impacts our lives in ways that we can't know or construe because they are multifarious and deeply hidden under the layers of life we are absorbed by and in. And there are constituent parts of our ecosystems that we simply don't have access to.

Recall: There have been times in the not so distant past when the way you 'felt' was different, possibly a close to the surface flow experience, or being in the zone, (remembering that 'flow' and 'in the zone' are different things), but something that connected you with an unusual feeling of perhaps being less self-aware and more connected to the life you were living. Recall what fulfilled you, for example, as distinct from what made you happy.

Happiness can be fleeting, but once satiated, the happiness may wane. An ice cream, for example, may indeed make you happy on a hot summers' day, but once satiated, your dopamine fix will quickly disappear as you hungrily search for the next fix to make you happy. On the other hand, if you are engaged in making the best artisan ice cream in the world – that enables you to live your values, connects you to a passion for great food and through your production of this fantastic ice cream, you start to make connections that lead you to building and extending a meaningful and significant network – you are more likely to be fulfilled. The fulfilment periods in your life represent times when your flow intensity was focused and close to, if not at its peak. Eudaimonia

Being able to recognise that friction in your life is not always a bad thing, it depends! And as such, being able to identify which kind of friction enables you and what friction triggers you and disables you is important for enhancing your flow capability. Ask about the labels you assign to others, to situations, and yourself; ask, 'Does the label enable?'

What friction is real and what is imagined; this is prevalent when we find ourselves trapped in past or future talk tracks, for example, 'if I hadn't done that yesterday' (past talk track) or 'what happens if the meeting goes badly tomorrow?' (future talk track). What kind of friction can you control, what can you influence, and what friction can't you control and therefore too much energy is wasted, and your flow diminished or diluted? Remember that where attention goes, energy flows.

Notice what you notice and then move your attention deliberately to what you think you may have missed. It's also worth revisiting the Goleman quote from earlier,

the range of what we think and do is limited by what we fail to notice, and because we fail to notice that we fail to notice, there is little we can do to change until we notice how failing to notice shapes our thoughts and deeds.

So, what are you failing to notice when it comes to friction and flow?

As we have learned, the one thing that people with high levels of flow in their lives seem to do is remember, recognise, reorder, and reorientate around people, place, sport, task, and activity quicker and with more resolve. They seem to curate their lives in a way that many people don't. People can be cognisant of how the weather impacts their flow, for example, vitamin D and just feeling the sunshine on your face is proven to heighten mood and the way we interact with others and our environment. Conversely, some people prefer the turning seasons, spring, and autumn, they use the seasons to leverage their flow. It's also worth remembering the Billy Connolly adage, 'There's no such thing as bad weather, only wrong clothes', so it's mind-shift again that enables.

As a coach, I notice that as I work with people on improving performance to enhance outcomes and intensify their flow, we spend time coaching for flow and in flow, and to do that they remember, recognise, reorder, and reorientate themselves towards flowfulness and a flow mind, working in and from the now, following a process to get to the outcome. These Rs are important because they are interesting and reflective in their nature.

I also use the following equation to enable people to think about their thinking, their metacognition if you like; $BQ + BA = BC$. Better questions + better answers = Better choices with stronger flow and resolve. This equation was developed for 10-year-old children in a primary school where the default question for them and teachers had become the ubiquitous, 'why?'. Instead, you could try, 'who, what, when, where, how?' as questions. It works, experiment with it. An example might be, 'why don't we recycle more at work?' no doubt you will meet with reasons and excuses, whereas if you ask, 'How might we recycle more?' you send the mind in a different direction.

I have added to this the idea that both in the societies and communities we belong to, which can be many and concurrent, as well as the general eco-systems we inhabit, flow can be diminished by the six Cs I consider dominant, although I am sure you will identify many other diminishing factors and forces. The six Cs include complicit, comply, conform, capitulate, collude, and coerced. For clarity, concurrent communities can include your family unit, your Alma Mata, your extended family i.e., the family you choose, your vocation, your employer's culture,

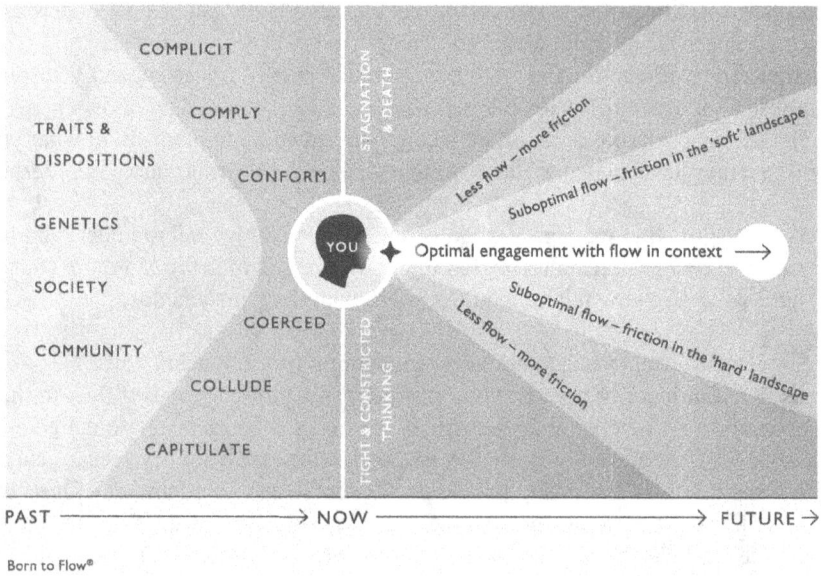

Figure 19.1 The constituents of your flow path

sports clubs you might belong to, amongst others – you are unlikely to belong to only one or exist in one ecosystem.

Figure 19.1 shows the constituents that inform the flow in your life.

Another way to consider the flow channel takes its inspiration from George Kelly, father of personal construct psychology or personal construct theory, as mentioned earlier on our journey down river.

If flow gets so tight and so constricted in its subjective construing, left of the channel in Figure 19.2, we might hypothesise that eventually it will become so tight, so constricted that it can't flow anymore, that the persons construing is no longer 'like water', the source has dried up, and ultimately, like a dry riverbed, life will cease to flourish there. No flow = dead.

On the far right of this channel, loose and dilated, we might consider that a person's construing is unable to focus with any intensity, and so numerous tributaries or interruptions overwhelm and overload their flow until it is so weakened that it becomes ineffective, transcends its own flow, and is lost in the estuarine environment of river meeting sea and gradually diluted until it is lost, literally, at sea.

We can see this in our everyday lives with the infinite variety of tech that could be contributing to our fulfilment and productivity and yet seems to endlessly beckon us towards a screen, large or small, and have us interact with endless amounts of content, not all of which adds value, and algorithms that mine deep into our psyche and as Johan Hari (2022) writes in his wonderful book *Stolen Focus*, 'I had just turned forty, and wherever my generation gathered, we would lament our lost capacity for concentration, as if it was a friend who had vanished one day at sea and never been seen since'.

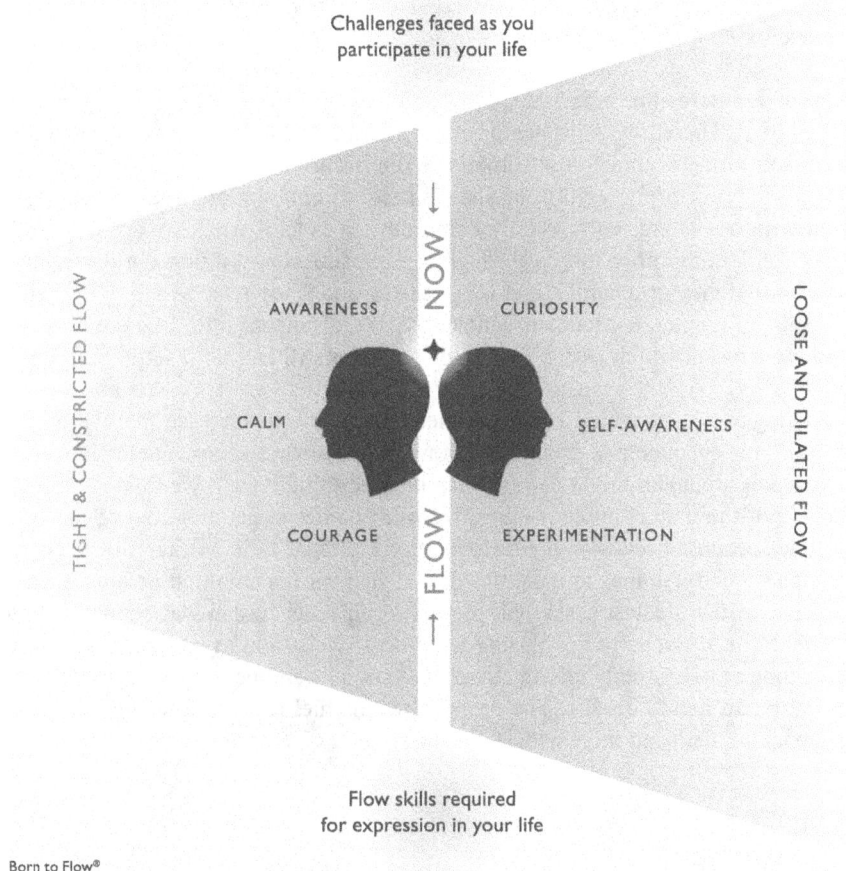

Challenges faced as you
participate in your life

TIGHT & CONSTRICTED FLOW

NOW

AWARENESS

CURIOSITY

CALM

SELF-AWARENESS

COURAGE

EXPERIMENTATION

FLOW

LOOSE AND DILATED FLOW

Flow skills required
for expression in your life

Born to Flow®

Figure 19.2 Keeping the flow channel balanced

Our focus may well have been misappropriated and our flow diluted, but not without us being complicit or colluding amongst other things. Flow demands a kind of vigilance, a certain devotion if you like to let it bring forth your potential into action in the now, a deep knowing and awareness that both grounds us in our being and lifts us above the ephemeral; the paradox of the flow being, perhaps. But then again, we are large; we contain multitudes.

For clarity, community can benefit us and vice versa. I repeat here George Bernard-Shaw's words from earlier,

I am of the opinion that my life belongs to the whole community and as long as I live, it is my privilege to do for it what I can. I want to be thoroughly used up when I die, for the harder I work, the more I live. I rejoice in life for its own sake. Life is no brief candle to me. It is a sort of splendid torch which I have got hold of for the moment and I want to make it burn as brightly as possible before handing it on to future generations.

What is interesting here is the way Shaw states, 'for the harder I work, the more I live'. There is a relationship between flow and friction that can be extrapolated from this, insomuch that sometimes the friction we encounter or create for ourselves deliberately, writing in Shaw's case, forcing a more attentive engagement with our being, will actually boost flow. It is as if when we are changing gears, generating more torque through the transmission through the drive, into the tires that they grip harder, and we go faster, and if we get it wrong, the wheels just spin and generate clouds of smoke that we disappear into, like the glass of muddy water, in which case it can be better to be still and let it settle before we move again.

Finding ways, of which I suggest there are many, to increase the use of the friction you encounter to boost your flow might at first seem counter intuitive, the counter argument might be that we train hard to fight easy, we train at altitude because of the impact on our bodies, we work harder to get more out of our life, our flow, because flow is an input to life, not an output of it. Michael Jordan is an exemplar when it comes to using friction as fuel for his ambition and drive. Perhaps one of the greatest basketball players of all time, Jordan was adept at using 'feedback' to drive more flow, using the most trivial slight to motivate him, even construing or deliberately misconstruing an action by another player or coach as an insult, to add fuel to his fire. The friction was his fuel for greatness, both internal and external, real, and imagined.

Summary

In this chapter, we see and consider:

- How you define, refine, and engage with your flow is within your gift.
- You can bond with your flow through integration and connecting with yourself and the ecosystem you live in.
- To integrate, we must align, and what we are aligning are differentiated elements within our sphere of influence and concern.
- Based on your sense making of flow and how it fits with your life and your engagement with it, create experiments and expand your thinking.
- The Rs are important because they are interesting and reflective in their nature. **Remembering.** As the conductor, Charles Hazlewood recalled, 'when I was young, I found all that flow. And then only to have it, kind of, completely drummed out of me with my first bloody and bruising encounters with the professional business'.
- **Recognising and retrieval**

Reconnecting

Recall: The fulfilment periods in your life represent times when your flow intensity was focused and close to, if not at its peak.

- Being able to recognise that friction in your life is not always a bad thing. Being able to identify the kind of friction that enables you and what triggers you and disables you is a critical skill.
- Remember that where attention goes, energy flows.
- BQ + BA = BC. Better questions + better answers = Better choices with stronger flow and resolve.
- Flow is diminished by the six Cs that can dominate: The six Cs include complicit, comply, conform, capitulate, collude, and coerced.
- Flow demands a kind of vigilance, a certain devotion if you like a deep knowing and awareness that both ground us in our being and lift us above the ephemeral.
- Find ways to increase the use of the friction you encounter to boost your flow: we train hard to fight easy; we train at altitude. Because of the impact on our bodies, we work harder to get more out of our life, our flow, as flow is an input to life expression.

Exercise/Reflective Practice

Ask yourself some check list questions consistently and remember Bill Walsh said, 'consistent effort is a consistent challenge'. These might include in no particular order:

1 Did I check in on my flow early enough today? (However, I measured it, if there was room for movement, was there room for improvement and, could I intensify my flow in relation to the day ahead i.e., living the day, not one task followed by another?)
2 Again, and often, ask yourself, does the 'label enable'?
3 Did I do everything within me to enable my best self to flow today?
4 Did I test how I might be flowing today?
5 Did I take the time to recognise how my flow was enabling me?
6 Was I willing to express myself through my flowfulness today?
7 Was I attentive to my flow throughout my endeavours today?
8 What labels have you adopted or given yourself that are sub-optimal for what you are trying to achieve?
9 Reflect on what labels you give others/situations and how you might reframe them to your advantage.

Reference

Hari, J. (2022). *Stolen focus: Why you can't pay attention–and how to think deeply again.* Crown Publishing Group.

Chapter 20

Teaching Flow

Currents

How early could we or should we teach people that they are born to flow and when can we start to teach kids that it is not time management that is important, but by definition, what they do with their time. It is attention *to their attention* that is key to them excelling and achieving, as McGilchrist (2018) so aptly describes in *Ways of Attending*. And as I've mentioned, where attention goes, energy flows.

Currently the prevailing education systems follow 'teach for the test' which ensures that the day is broken down into lessons, which are broken down into segments, and again these are broken down into minutes, which are focussed on the teacher following the stated curriculum in a certain amount of time. How often do you recall hearing the refrain that 'there wasn't much time left' or 'why haven't you finished?' or 'why are you doing that?', or 'why haven't you done it yet?'. The 'why?' question is guaranteed to interrupt your story, artwork, science, maths, and your flow. Earlier we talked of my equation, $BQ + BA = BC$, for the very reasons outlined above.

Rarely do I remember, during the course of a lesson hearing, a teacher ask, 'where is your attention'. That phrase is obfuscated by the familiar refrain of 'are you paying attention' which elicits a binary response, usually mumbled or nothing at all, a response in itself. And the question usually refers to the teachers' words, their authority, the whiteboard, or blackboard if you are old enough to remember them, and the task being done. Seldom does it refer to the activity of paying attention to your attention, such that you might know where you are in flowing through the activity, attentive to the joy of your life, expressing itself through following your flow as it takes you through the lesson.

And we may well recall when we were in the presence of a teacher, that was in flow and that it enabled our flow. I certainly remember teachers who held classes gripped with their ability to make their subject relevant, interesting, exciting, building a flow confluence. I also remember the command-and-control teachers who lost the class before the children entered the classroom. And in talking to teachers over the last few years, I've been told many times that they feel unsupported, under-valued, over-worked, and under-paid, more importantly, teaching isn't what they thought it would be. Let's be honest, teaching is a tough gig.

DOI: 10.4324/9781351169929-22

The spaces and places which lessons flow through and which a child could flow through the lessons, are constantly interrupted by the need for authority to command attention, rather than let attention command authority. An interesting way to think about this might be through the time sheet or the timetable.

A time sheet allegedly measures what you have done with your time; a timetable tells you where you should be at any given time; and a watch tells you what time it isn't; that's why you check it so often. The first two are ultimately concerned with outputs and activity, but neither measure where your attention was in relation to the activity you were undertaking whilst using these 'tools'. And we should not simply pass over the fact, that people, especially command and control leaders, mistake activity for productivity, so we may well be measuring the wrong thing. As mentioned the baseball player, Michael Kopech wears a watch that says, 'NOW', so that he stays with and in the moment.

The time sheet, for example, does not measure how much flow you were experiencing (except in experiments that are trying to name flow), or joy, frustration. It doesn't care for your mindset or mental state at any given moment; it merely records what was done and how many billable minutes can be attributed to a certain task. The body of data is therefore only measuring the outputs associated with the task and not the human inputs. It doesn't understand, like most algorithms, for example, that when you started the activity you may have paid attention to your flow and noticed that it was ebbing around a 2 or 3, it cannot record that in noticing this you asked yourself a question, something like 'what can I do to increase my flow, where can I put my attention during this activity?'. The time sheet, in this form, is an enemy of productivity, creativity, and the increasing of flow.

Flow offers an opportunity, with regard to learning, that may address the balance in the way that our early experiences in life are overrepresented in our memory because of the sheer number of learning opportunities, as described earlier by Claudia Hammond, that occur in our formative years. Flow learning at any stage in life, with a flow mind-shift, might enable us to embed those deep learning sequences for several reasons, not least of all what's going on chemically in our brains at times of critical learning, but the state of our whole being, at any age, learning something of interest and importance, meaningful and significant, which lends itself to good brain health through neural plasticity.

And there's a simple message here, if you codify education to nothing more than certification, there are many things that may slip through the net, and an innate understanding of one's ability to flow might be one of them.

Summary

In this chapter, we consider and try to make sense of:

- In context, the 'why?' question is almost guaranteed to interrupt your story, artwork, science, math, and your flow. Obviously in specific enquiry into the nature of things, for example, we will always ask 'why?'.

- Command-and-control is the flightpath to extinction.
- **Tools** aren't sentient and by definition the 'relationship' is input/output. The tool doesn't understand how you might use it to flow.
- If we codify education to nothing more than certification, there are many things will slip through the net, and an innate understanding of one's ability to flow will be one of them.

Exercise/Reflective Practice

1 The simple practice of noticing others flowing is a learning opportunity.
2 The practice of facilitating others to increase their flow is also something of a learning opportunity. Getting kids to enjoy their flow is easier because there will be less resistance. What kind of space do you think you could curate to generate more flow?
3 Cultivate the practice of paying attention to your attention.

Reference

McGilchrist, I. (2018). *Ways of attending: How our divided brain constructs the world.* Routledge.

Chapter 21

The Flow Mind-Shift

Tributary

'We are not thinking machines that feel, we are feeling machines that think', so said António Damásio.. In relation to flow, this is a key differentiator when construing the flow mind, the flow body, and the spirit of flow. Perhaps those 37 trillion+ cells in your body, pulsating, flowing, enabling, are helping you feel your way to thinking about flow. Listening to your mind and feeling how your body expresses itself in moving and aligning to a direction of travel, through feeling its way forward through the terrain of life, across the riverbed step by step, is a slightly different way to make sense of your flow mind and perhaps conjoins with flow as a way of being. As Alan Watts (2011, p. 47) cites Lao Tzu in *Tao: The Watercourse Way*, 'Nothing in the world is weaker than water, but it has no better in overcoming the hard'.

A flow mind-shift is one of being open to the idea that flow is related to our being, not our relationship with doing. As historian Arnold Toynbee is credited with saying. 'Those who think history is just one damn thing after another', could have been talking about trying to reach flow through finding the tasks that sets flow up, the canonical belief made real by association with task. It could be the wrong way around; flow enables us to express through the task and enables to push steadily through our subjective range of flow being, refining, tuning, reflecting on our flow in the moment.

And as the Buddhist sage, Yamamoto Tsunetomo (2012) wrote in *Hagakure*, 'Live being true to the single purpose of the moment', and in that one perfectly formed sentence you step closer to living in your flow. The time is always now; the way is always flow.

We have covered how remembering, recall, and retrieval enable us to connect and align with our flow at a deeper level than we might do currently.

Watching elite athletes, who are only human (hard to believe sometimes I know), is a good way to watch flow-being increase during the course of a day and then return to resting or recovery flow. Being an elite athlete is definitely a way of being; wake up sore being an athlete, getting to training through heavy traffic, still being an athlete, starting the warmups as an elite athlete, into drills as an elite athlete, and all the time moving through flow progression, till completely at home in the flow, expressing your best self through your flow capacity and

DOI: 10.4324/9781351169929-23

then unwinding back through the flow to recovery and resting in the natural great flow that can aid our healing and recuperation. It's an easy lesson to learn that recovery is a flow endeavour too, but it's from the need of your being, not a task to accomplish.

In talking about our hypothetical athlete above, we are setting up an intellectual encounter with someone who could be using flow throughout their lives. Intellectual encounters with flow, rather than experiential ones, have led to the canonical idea of flow as a 'mental state', a state to get into, and this has become the norm and most academic responses/experiments seem aimed at verifying that; looking where the light is, as previously stated. A mental state, for our purposes, can be considered the condition of the mind at a given point in time. It takes into account what you think or what you feel: Distraction or focus, for example. But this, according to some interpretations, can only be inferred, an epistemic approach, whereby actions may betray someone's mental state and give insight as to what is really going on.

Again, Kelly (2003) is useful here when we consider flow, 'The fact that these constructs are clinicians constructs of clients constructs may have caused the reader some difficulty', he writes in *The Psychology of Personal constructs*, talking about how we should consider the psychologists determination of what might be going on for someone.

Flow transcends the labelling of a singular 'mental-state' because with experience, practice, and a recognition of what flow might be, you can start increasing the intensity and focus of feeling and living your flow. It can be further embedded as a mindset, although I prefer the term, 'mind-shift'; your way of being. And as Carol Dweck (2017) writes, 'a growth mindset is about believing people can develop their abilities. It's that simple'. In the born to flow approach, you recognise flow as your way of being, in perhaps the same way someone embraces zen, stoicism, ikigai, or the Tao; it enables you to explore the boundaries of your potential, to further own your unique flow.

Mindset is, according to OED Online, Oxford University Press, an 'established set of attitudes, especially regarded as typical of a particular group's social or cultural values'. Mind-set then is, in a sense, the contents of the mind and it's construing, and we tend to think of it as a modern idiom, however we can trace it back to the early 20th century, with popularity beginning to rise in around 1980; it turns out we've been thinking about 'mindset' for a long time. And we've been thinking about the 'act of flowing' since about 1420 AD (Chambers, 2002, p. 394).

Mindset can be a choice if you have been enabled and equipped to make it so; it depends on many variables, but it can be taught. Perhaps then, we exist on a continuum mindset, or better still, mind-shifts, from perhaps fixed to growth, for example, or in a vaguely Kellian way, from tight and constricted mindset through to a looser and more dilated one, a bit more flexible in our cognition. Accordingly, if you can shift your mind, and by definition your thinking and your construing, from what you have been told 'flow' *is*, to what you might own and construe flow *as*, you shift your fulfilment, happiness, and performance along that continuum and hold it there, through owning it and not capitulating to the flow orthodoxy.

The flow mind-shift is helped by just simply noticing where you are at any given moment in your flow, however, to construe or take ownership of it. To simply notice and not necessarily do anything with what you notice, just let it flow through your mind. It's so much harder than we realise to just notice without opinion or naming or judgement.

If you see a tree swaying in the breeze, there is always a part of your super-consciousness trying to name it, and frame it against some background. Is it this tree or that tree, what is the wind speed making it sway, is there a nest in it, how old is it? And in all those enquiries, it's difficult just to be with the tree, noticing. An ancient Chinese proverb springs to mind here, 'is the tree moving, is the wind moving, is the mind moving?'.

Often in the process of writing this book, I've noticed that the words flow from somewhere else, from a distant point of reference, or inspiration or nature, or near memory, or tariki. And sometimes I'm pulled deeper into my flow as the words become a torrent and sometimes, I notice that my flow is calling me to slow and reflect and trickle a little whilst something else goes on in my absorption and distillation of my flow thoughts.

The noticing rarely gets in the way of either thinking, doing, or being, though I do not give myself easily to the many distractions. But this too is a mind-shift.

For example, I am much more conscious of my mobile phone accompanying me through life, as I imagine more people are today, and I notice deliberately when it is a tool and when it is a distraction. This is very different to the early use of my phone, when all the notifications were switched on and I knew when I got an e-mail or a text, or someone tagged me on LinkedIn or Instagram, and now occasionally the phone rings, which is the only notification I get, and mostly that's on silent because the caller can leave a message.

In noticing, without trying to do something about what I notice in my flow, I found my flowfulness became a more constant and consistent companion, especially when other stuff was *flowing* around me. And sometimes it's just movement, sometimes it's elite performance, sometimes it's just people being optimal in their moment. I let the noticing come and go, letting my super-consciousness store away the things that were interesting or important about my dynamic, complex, psychological, flow process. I gave my flow room to flow without the need to always name or rate the experience, giving faith to the flow, not the dogma attached to it. I also notice that when I'm flowing at my best, it's because I'm overflowing, something has to get out, the perfect swim at dawn, a haiku, a great coaching session, not because something is trying to get in, as it were.

I know there's that chicken and egg situation again; does the perfect swim at dawn bring out my flow or is it the fact that I get my backside out of bed to go for the swim, that the flow wants to emerge in that swim? And what got me out of bed, was it the outcome, that wasn't promised, of the perfect swim at dawn, or was it something inside me? Make of it what you will, and to paraphrase the legendary basketball coach, Pat Summitt, your flow is what it is. But it will be what you make it.

And more importantly the greatest mind-shift over the last 20 years or so has been to give myself permission to know that I flow, I'm surfing the flux, at ease with this natural experience, knowing that I would be hyper-focussed whilst working with a client and in flow and sometimes lost in a timeless reverie whilst laying by the ocean or a river, where time slowed down, I was fulfilled by the sounds of the water gurgling, the guls screeching, the birds singing, the wind in the waves, in the trees, and I lost my self-awareness to that moment and found a oneness with the environment, and I emerged some later time fulfilled and refreshed. Time had flown, whilst I slowed down, whilst the earth spun on.

I have previously written, published on the professional networking site, LinkedIn, about why we get knocked down nine times but get up ten, and the only explanation that rings true for me, in my construing, is that I have not finished with life, and that allows me to get back up.

And life is not a task to complete; otherwise it might be over too soon. It is, in my eyes, non-purposive, and it is the 'doing' of it itself that is important and we do that from a place of being, as Alan Watts might have described it, in the same way he considered both music and dance, you don't dance to reach a particular place on the dance floor or play music to reach the end as fast as possible.

Aligning yourself as best as you can to the bio-psycho-social-environmental and technological aspects of your life is likely to extend your flow into more of your endeavours. There is no division between the internal and the external, in terms of the river or stream as it flows through its surroundings, it does not know it is 'other'; it is part of.

This is not an uncommon way of construing the way we can exist in the world, a oneness, like the fish in the Alan Watts quote earlier or as he further says in a lecture,

> we leave out of our everyday consciousness, one amazing beauty of experience that we never see at all, and on the other hand, a very deep thing the sense of our basic identity, unity with, oneness with, the total process of being.

He could have said, the process of flowing.

I think that it is when we limit our flow through outmoded beliefs, following unhealthy dogma, limiting ourselves, and a corrupt mindset, that the slow descent towards stagnation begins and as we know, stagnation is followed by death. And because this can happen slowly, over a long period of time, we tend not to notice that we are coming inexorably to a place where we do ourselves more damage because, as stated earlier, we stopped daring and started caring about what the world thought we are capable of, and as David Foster Wallace (1997) wrote in *Infinite Jest*, 'You will become way less concerned with what other people think of you when you realize how seldom they do'.

The mind-shift required is to realise that one's will to flow is not essential, and to paraphrase Watts from earlier, when 'your will is exhausted, you've tried everything to make something work & it won't work, and then to achieve the perfection of the art (flow), something has to happen of itself'; well flow is a happening of itself. And as Vincent Walsh, Professor of Brain Research at University College London, said during our conversation, 'Actually, given the paucity of our fundamental learning I think it would be much better to put 99% of your effort into learning whatever it is you do and let the flow be an emergent property'.

For clarity, 'Emergent properties arise from the interaction of factors or items in a high-level system which, as a result, has qualities possessed by none of the individual factors' according to Desmond et al. (2019).

And so, the born to flow diagram (Figure 5.1) shows that the interaction of the identified elements, once understood, aligned, and fully associated with, can produce a deepness to our emergent property of flow. In other words, the flow mind-shift occurs when the sum total of the internal and external are so in tune, integrated, and aligned that the boundaries that we think divide us, from this and that, us and them, state and non-state, fade away and leave us with only a knowing of flow as a dynamic, complex psychological process that we have shifted to at a super-conscious level. We are in the groove.

Summary

In this chapter, we consider:

- 'We are not thinking machines that feel, we are feeling machines that think' to António Damásio.
- 'Nothing in the world is weaker than water, but it has no better in overcoming the hard' according to Lao-Tzu.
- The flow mind is one (the mind) of being open to the idea that flow is related to our being, not our relationship with our doing'
- Recovery is a flow endeavour too, it is not necessarily a task to accomplish.
- Intellectual encounters with flow, rather than experiential ones, have led to the idea of flow as a 'mental state'. It's mimetic.
- A mental state can be considered the condition of the mind at a given point in time.
- Flow transcends the labelling of 'mental state' because with experience, practice, and recognition, you can start increasing the intensity and focus of feeling your flow.
- 'A growth mindset is about believing people can develop their abilities. It's that simple' according to Carol Dweck.
- In the born to flow approach, you recognise flow as your way of being, and it can enable you to further explore the boundarylessness of your potential.
- Mind-set then is, in a sense, the contents of the mind and it's construing.
- Mind-shift can be a choice.
- Own your flow and do not capitulate to the flow orthodoxy.
- The flow mind-shift is helped by just simply noticing where you are at any given moment in your flow.

- It's much harder than we realise to just notice, without opinion/naming/judgement.
- Give yourself permission to know that you were in flow, surfing the flux, at ease with this natural experience.
- Aligning yourself to the bio-psycho-social-environmental and technological aspects of your life is more likely to extend your flow into your endeavours.
- The river, as it flows through its surroundings, does not know it is 'other' than.
- Emergent properties arise from the interaction of factors or items in a high-level system which, as a result, has qualities possessed by none of the individual factors.

Exercise/Reflective Practice

1 If we are not thinking machines that feel, but are feeling machines that think, practice thinking about how you feel in relation to your thoughts.
2 Reflect on whether you think of rest and recovery as a flow endeavour, from the need of your being, and not just a task to accomplish. Reflect on how you prepare to rest and whether your sleep protocols enable rest and recovery, optimally.
3 Consider how often you just notice, without opinion or naming or judgement. To name is to intellectualise and not everything needs that to happen.

References

Chambers, A. (2002). *The chambers dictionary*. Allied Publishers.
Desmond, C., Seeley, J., Groenewald, C., Ngwenya, N., Rich, K., & Barnett, T. (2019). Interpreting social determinants: Emergent properties and adolescent risk behaviour. *PLoS One, 14*(12), e0226241.
Dweck, C. (2017). *Mindset-updated edition: Changing the way you think to fulfil your potential*. Hachette, UK.
Kelly, G. A. (2003). A brief introduction to personal construct theory. In F. Fransella (Ed.), International handbook of personal construct psychology (pp. 3–20). John Wiley & Sons Ltd.
Tsunetomo, Y. (2012). *Hagakure: The book of the samurai*. Shambhala Publications.
Wallace, D. F. (1997). *Infinite jest*. Abacus.
Watts, A. (2011). *Tao: The watercourse way*. Souvenir Press.

Chapter 22

Confluence

Flowing Together

A confluence is the point where two rivers meet, where the power merges and they continue on the journey as one body of water pushing towards the ocean, towards a bigger thing, more than the sum total of the parts. The metaphor still holds if people can join in endeavours, as members of a team or real community, as partners, as innovators or inventors, teachers, collaborators, or coaches, then the potential builds and it can build towards a flow experience that may be shared.

No two people will experience flow in the same way; we know it's subjective. Science tells us that much in the same way no two people ever read the same book, or step into the same river and indeed, no person can ever step into the same river twice. However, they can experience flow at the same time if they understand it is available to them. They may express the flow through social constructivism, the journey of collaborative learning into the new areas to be explored when two or more energies join.

If understanding that you are born to flow enables you in some way to reach further into the reserves of your potential, and that in turn brings you closer to your undiscovered potential and enables you to achieve more as your life develops in its complexity, then sharing that in team performance or community, for example, is a natural extension of that existential experience.

Understanding that a group of people does not necessarily make a team, we should nevertheless explore how one introduces the idea that a confluence flow may occur in a group of people, whether elite athletes or a team in business, or perhaps children learning together.

If this book is about anything, it's about potential and flow in individuals. Perhaps it is with the integration and alignment of the many aspects of our psychological selves, and the elements suggested earlier that we share with others in our quest for deep fulfilment and to live life purposefully, to achieve more, that we truly commune with our best selves in flow.

In born to flow terms what might that look like? The flow experience is so subjective that it might present more barriers to breakthrough if we compare our constructs. Confluence of energy in a shared experience of flow might be what unlocks our collective and collaborative potential further by enabling us to let go, as it were.

There are certain fundamental truths about working with others that are well known, for example, establishing ways of working (WoW), getting to know, trust

DOI: 10.4324/9781351169929-24

and believe in each other, from acting randomly to acting with intent, moving from the individuals capability to seeing the collective potential of confluent flow, from having separate identities in the endeavour to embracing a shared team or group identity that has focus, moving from frustration to participating in making things better, understanding that you are colleagues in a process, suspending assumptions and being able to have generative dialogue that enables further discovery. And to do this with others who understand they were born to flow, or who are at least willing to test the hypothesis by adopting some flow practice. And those who are willing to embrace the beginners mind or empty their cup. Further, through the lens of what is right with this confluence of flow energy, rather than what is wrong or missing, this might accelerate the process that leads to a collective, collaborative flow.

Perhaps you have worked on a project with a group of people who were equally committed to discovering their best selves through navigating and solving a complex issue – attentive to the issue but also attentive to the way you collaborated – because as we have discovered, where attention goes, energy flows; so the opportunity to flow through an experience of complex problem solving by having cognisance of yours and others flow can enable a mind-shift.

Summary

In this chapter, flowing together we see:

- A confluence is the point where two rivers meet.
- When people join in endeavours, as members of a team, as partners, as innovators or inventors, teachers, or coaches, then the potential builds and it can build towards a flow experience that may be shared.
- No two people experience flow in the same way; however, they can experience flow at the same time if they understand it is available to them.
- A journey of collaborative learning emerges when two or more energies join.
- Flow can enable you to reach further into the reserves of your potential and that can bring you closer to undiscovered potential.
- A group of people does not necessarily make a team (obvious but true), but a confluence flow may occur in a group of people.
- Confluence of energy to a shared experience of flow might be what unlocks our collective and collaborative potential.
- To discover your flow it helps to embrace the beginner's mind.
- To flow through the experience of complex problem solving by having cognisance of yours and others flow can enable a mind-shift.

Exercise/Reflective Practice

1 Perhaps the key to confluence is to notice when it is arising amongst a group of people; it might be a shift in energy that you notice. Reflect on the subtle differences, the tiny margins between a group working well together and a team being equally committed to each other and the journey and, what they are becoming. Identifying these differences might enable you to associate it with your construing of flow.

Chapter 23

The Campaign

Anabranch

In adding to and broadening of the definition of flow, we rub up against the complexity of being, and this is as it should be. We shouldn't be trying to simplify life or flow; both are complex, dynamic, psychological processes. As mentioned earlier, the idea that there are cheat sheets for every subject or life hacks for the difficulties encountered demeans the experience of being and doing that pushes our boundaries beyond the horizon of our known worlds. In the continuing exploration of our own experiences, which might be thought of as 'a campaign', we are gaining deep knowledge and wisdom about ourselves. It is important at times to become our own iconoclast, not least to challenge the wisdom we receive unquestioningly as well as our own assumptions, constructs, and beliefs.

The Indian philosopher, Jiddu Krishnamurti said, 'The more you know yourself, the more clarity there is. Self-knowledge has no end – you don't come to an achievement; you don't come to a conclusion. It is an endless river'. Again the river unfolds within us, and flow is ubiquitous in most philosophical thought.

And so it is with the following pages, they are like an outdated map, a sat-nav that hasn't had its software updated. They are impregnated with my construing, my flow experiences, my iconoclastic rebellion against my acquired knowledge. And whilst there might be signposts for you as you seek to understand and uncover the beauty and power of your flow, that is all they can ever be.

The physiological concomitants of my flow experience, for example, may measure differently to yours; an EEG of my brain activity in flow may well be different to yours; my heart may slow in flow, yours may quicken; respiratory differences may be identified between your flow and mine, but it doesn't denigrate my flow or yours.

We have spoken about the ability to retrieve an experience that we might describe as somewhat like flow, especially during formative or early years as a way of reconnecting with flow. Our inhibitions about what flow might be should not become a barrier to the breakthrough in our flow performance based on another's interpretation. We must reconnect with our own experience or our belief in our own possibility to flow constantly and consistently.

I believe there is a way. As I write this tributary of the book, I am recovering from bi-lateral hip replacement, Birmingham Hip Resurfacing to be precise, the

DOI: 10.4324/9781351169929-25

most widely used hip replacement procedure in the world. There have been complications post operatively. As one might expect with any major surgery, it is complex,
and if we define complexity as something that has interdependency, multiplicity, is
dynamic, and has diversity, there's more than enough opportunity for things to go
awry. My surgeon is eminent, but I got a wound infection – it happens. My physio
is a former lead physio at a major rugby club in the UK. He's used to dealing with
trauma, but there are complications. I am eight months post-operative, and the pain
has been between moderate and excruciating, between uncomfortable and debilitating. I have been challenged to flow with all these frictions, and it works really
well when I am focussed on flowing through the trauma, not on the outcome of
relieving the pain.

It relaxes me to work with the healing, as in our hypothetical athlete mentioned
earlier, using flow in recovery, enabling mind to work with body not against it,
through anxiety or boredom, not resisting through frustration because it hasn't gone
quite right, straight away. And as I tune into the pain, the healing, the complexity,
the remembering, the retrieval of the power of flow I have a deeper understanding
of myself, my self-concept as a patient, co-conspirator in the exploration of my hip
replacement as a test for flowfulness.

You may describe this as a simple reframing of the problem, but it is so much
more than that because I realise that even when not hyper-focussed on the hips I
am in flow, I have diverted the energy I would use when one is in constant pain
to a place where it can be used to continue to function effectively and efficiently
through life whilst the recovery flows on. Perhaps, this is an example of what Csikszentmihalyi thought of as micro-flow; again, it's subjective.

I wrote the following during a spell in a rehabilitation hospital many years ago,
before I had started to expand my definition of flow or questioned the canonical
flow orthodoxy. I had already started to construe my way of being as a way to flow:

Unsted Park Diary – Songs of Pain in Linear Time: 11 June and 12 June 2000

Today I begin to search for what are euphemistically known here as 'Baselines'.
It actually means reducing life into the number of seconds before pain begins in
any given situation. I have tried to explain that I am never without pain. My an-
ger is at them (medical team), at me, at the frustration of time. If I live in linear
time, that is to say, if I measure *pain* in ordinary time, in these baselines, then I
am condemned to a life lived in seconds.

A life lived with one eye on the ticking clock, listening to a body that has
learned to live outside normal time frames so as to accommodate pain, and one
that will now be wading through the hours towards an inevitable end. Linear
moments move pain along from second to second by recognition of its existence
and this concept is alien to all I have learnt about pain and time.

Yet, if I continue to move through pain, denying its gnawing presence,
not accepting it, I run the risk of finding myself beached in ordinary time

anyway. Am I then to find a way to live an ordinary life in an extra-ordinary way?

This then is the song of pain in ordinary time, sung in the silent cathedral of a body that has learnt to live in denial of pain and at the same time is held captive by it – a song out of time, discord, without cadence, without end. It is a song I can no longer allow myself to sing.

Unsted Park Diary – Past, Present, and Future Tense: 27 June 2000

At last, I am beginning to understand what I have always known, that I am able to add to the infinite variety of tools that I have acquired during my life to help me continue to reclaim my life. I always knew it, but I needed help to fully understand it.

I can see that even the tools that I must now discard have been useful and without them I would not have travelled this far. Thus, even as they are discarded, they are useful in a past kind of memory tense.

Even now I am reconciled to the fact that there will be greater and lesser pain – more tears. I can see I am always at the beginning in journeying alongside the pain, that we are inseparable in present tense. The past is a place of reference not residence, as Roy T. Bennet quipped.

Future tense is an illusion, as yet unlived. It is soon to come or long ago – my memories no longer cling, my visualisations no longer grasp.

I am ready for whatever may arise in the sunrise of tomorrow or from the mists of yesterday. What pain has come will be released by right mindedness, the application of technique and understanding the now. The journey never ends. The tools are available. The time is now.

Ends

As I reflect on the diary excerpt above, I have a sense that I was rediscovering a way of being that had been lost to me, that I was born to flow, and that *it is* a way of being. Something else started to emerge during the confinement in the rehabilitation hospital, and that was learning to see the happiness and fulfilment in each moment and start to understand that *it is flow* – no matter that the deep pain and all the other concomitants, the frustration, the debilitation, the impatience, the feeling of inadequacy, the sense of grief for the life that was slipping away from me, were overwhelming me and overloading me at times. I saw the glimmer that the small gains, and they were very small at times, were moments that I could be happy in and with.

I have learnt that being with flow is an enabler of resilience; it specifically enables us to recover quickly from setbacks or difficulties, withstand upsets and the everyday frictions that we encounter. To fully flow in any moment, bringing your whole self to the point in time where you truly are, is to stand four square to the situation, whatever the context, however uncomfortable, be with the circumstance (which has its roots in the 'surrounding condition'), and to understand that each moment offers an opportunity that we will weight, according to our likes and pre-dispositions, our learning and our biases; we are never in that moment alone unless we have dedicated, like Yamamoto Tsunetomo, ourselves to actualising and uncovering, as Martin Buber suggests, 'As I actualise, I uncover'.

We may frame resilience in many ways – mental toughness, grit, mindset. We will construe it based on our experience of it or lack of. Again, I think of resilience as a complex, dynamic psychological process, one that we can train for, one that sometimes just naming it, as Professor Mark Wilson suggests, may give us what we need in that single moment to overcome or transcend, to get through or move beyond. Some of you may be familiar with the Japanese proverb, 'knocked down seven times stand up eight' (nana korobi ya oki) or a version of it. We can construe it in many ways, but to me it speaks to seeing what is beyond the moment that has floored us and so we rise; it speaks to never giving up; and it speaks to resilience, mental toughness, vision, and grit.

I have always believed that I get back up because I know I have not finished, there is more to be, to do, to become. There is the inevitability that one day I will not get back up, it may not be of my choosing, but whilst I believe I have not finished and whilst I am able, my flow will enable me to rise.

Summary

In this chapter, we consider:

- Broadening the definition, interpretation, and construing of flow is something to be embraced.
- The exploration of our own experiences of flow might be thought of as a campaign.
- 'The more you know yourself, the more clarity there is. Self-knowledge has no end – you don't come to an achievement; you don't come to a conclusion. It is an endless river' according to Jiddu Krishnamurti.
- You must constantly update your 'flow' mapping/sat-nav. Maps have been used for thousands of years and enable us to identify the terrain we are in, remembering as *Alfred Korzybski* said, 'the map is not the territory'.
- Our inhibitions about what flow might be should not become a barrier to the breakthrough in our flow performance based on another's interpretation.
- We must reconnect with our own experience and our belief to flow constantly and consistently.
- Be focussed on flowing through the trauma (friction) not on the outcome.
- Being with flow is an enabler of resilience; it specifically enables us to recover quickly from setbacks or difficulties, withstand upsets and the everyday frictions that we encounter.
- Martin Buber suggests, 'As I actualize, I uncover'.

Exercise/Reflective Practice

1 Deep exploration of times that we have overcome some kind of adversity in our lives, either with guidance or through our own undertaking is a worthwhile exercise. To be able to draw learning from the experience and use it to evolve as we unfold our life on the landscapes we inhabit can be enabling. Consider times you have overcome some form of adversity and how it informs your development and evolution and could increase your flow. Again, formalise this through writing it down, painting, drawing, and connect the brain in many ways to the subconscious mind.

Chapter 24

A Way of Being

Returning to the Source

Being mindful of what you are doing in the moment can include deep reflection on past matters without mindless reverie or planning for the future without the mind-numbing anxiety or fear of consequences, without daydreaming.

How then to be happy, and further, fulfilled in the moment, would perhaps be better considered as how to be happy *with* the moment; there is a difference.

The way to flow *is* to flow, that is, feel the flow, get lost in your own inner being, and move gradually outwards as you understand the simple sophistication of your being, drinking upstream as it were, returning to the source that, has to date, enabled you to get this far in life, but cognisant of the now well-known Marshall Goldsmith aphorism, 'what got you here won't get you there'. To be the flow you have to become the flow, to paraphrase Bruce Lee.

If the way to flow is to exercise flow muscles as it were, we should exercise appropriately and the way we might think about this is to develop a deep awareness of how we generally exist within ourselves and within the world.

We have talked about mindset, but I sense that flow can be a bypass of the conscious mind, an intuitive experience of our way of being rather than an always deliberate move towards or away from a task. Intuition sits lightly on the shoulder of intellect, and I think is closely related to a way of being. When intuition is allowed room in our mind we generally tend to *think* about issues, problems, and opportunities in a different way. We cut loose from the procedures and processes, we attune to something deeper that exists within us and, often when we tune into something that is going on or we have intuitive thought or insight, it is akin to a flow experience.

Indeed, Jeff Grout says this of flow, 'part of it is tied up with the fact that you're not thinking, that you're doing things completely intuitively', and Justin Hughes offered the idea that, 'is it a sort of symbiotic thing that as it (task) starts to go well, the mindset improves, and the mindset improves the task?' It's an interesting idea and one that we should consider, if we have an adaptable mindset that can react well under pressure, for example, and in the moment, we see improvement and from there, we gain traction and the task gets better and the outcome is great, does one go hand in hand with the other? We might cultivate an adaptability to our mindset, or as Dweck proposes 'a growth mindset', that enables performance gains. It's not that the mindset is positive or upbeat all the time; we might recognise when we could

DOI: 10.4324/9781351169929-26

be better and adjust. Red2Blue performance under pressure is an excellent tool for this. This points back to exercising the flow muscle, just tuning into your flow will increase it in the moment, and get you used to the feeling that it's there, on tap.

Intuition is a trait that we all have, probably a human universal, and when we experience it, we know we have been intuitive before, we know we are being intuitive in the moment, and we know we will be intuitive again. It's the same with flow, if we register that we have had flow experiences, then we can, through our practice, retrieve that latent power from within us. Herbert Simon (1992) thought this of intuition, 'The situation has provided a cue; this cue has given the expert access to information stored in memory, and the information provides the answer. Intuition is nothing more and nothing less than recognition'.

This points to the idea that experiences of flow are retrievable. Had we encoded flow when we were young, it would be much easier to bring that 'super-power' to the fore. And if we accept the premise that we are born to flow, then it points to the opportunities that it affords us, not least of all, the anticipatory predictiveness when our flow is at its zenith, when thinking is too slow for us to be optimal, and effortless effort releases us from the thinking mind so that we flow beyond our bounded rationality. (It should be noted that intuition is probably not a scientifically proven resource for making decisions, and that if it is indeed just recognition, we need to be attentive to the falsity of patterns emerging that cause us to think we are being intuitive based on an inexact replication: An attribution of our intuitive insight the first time in context being wrong because the context changed and our mindset did not.)

And with diligence and devotion, raising our awareness around our flow experiences, one day we will find that the *trying* has ceased, and the flow way is a constant companion. Having deep awareness and connectedness to our flow or micro-flow moments, to the single purpose of the way, of being in that moment and, then expanding those moments out gradually into longer periods of time is within us, not preordained by a canonical belief in a prerequisite number of constituent elements.

By definition, we interact with the external world through the things that we must do, the things we choose to do, and sometimes the things we are forced to do. The internal and external are inextricably linked. As Alan Watts posits, 'Your skin does not separate you from the world. It's a bridge through which the external world flows into you. And you flow into it'. There is always interaction across boundaries and borders, some of which are real and some imagined, but all of which make up the human experience, and to emphasise, it is our proactivity and reactivity to both internal and external stimuli that combine to give us more than the sum total of each moment.

Curiosity and gratitude, for example, are enablers to be happy *with* the moment. And we return again to Yamamoto Tsunetomo,

There is surely nothing other than the single purpose of the present moment. A man's whole life is a succession of moment after moment. There will be nothing else to do, and nothing else to pursue. Live being true to the single purpose of the moment.

For most people today, this is lost to the cacophony of interruption stolen focus from the moment. It's the habit of our mind to wander towards whatever it thinks is calling for it to pay attention. when it is our mind that should discern what is worthy of our attention, where we should allow our energy to focus, and with what level of intensity.

Being *with* the moment requires an understanding that it will pass. So relishing it, being fully present in it, or placing it in perspective is the only way to have the most with that moment, before it is lost, gone, too late to recall it and worse, to know that we blew it, we will not have 'that' moment again, as Martha Graham, the acclaimed choreographer, wrote,

> There is a vitality, a life force, an energy, a quickening that is translated through you into action, and because there is only one of you in all time, this expression is unique. And if you block it, it will never exist through any other medium and will be lost.

This can only happen with the purpose of the moment fully in mind habitually. And whilst this might sound exhausting, it is merely a better way of being that one can reclaim from the tyranny of intrusion.

Being fulfilled within the moment is facilitated by being mindful of our tendency towards other things on near or far horizons. Called by the Sirens towards the rocks of distraction, we must see ourselves seeing the AND being the lighthouse. So, alongside curiosity and gratitude, we must cultivate a mind that is mindful of itself and still be with the moment.

We might do this by meditative practice; however, you construe meditation; for me it can be as simple as breathing, sometimes box breathing, sometimes just picking a random number and counting down each time I breathe out. The count on the out breath brings me back to my focus of a quiet mind. I often lose myself in the 'micro-flow' of 'house beautification', commonly known as housework, but the simple act of being with the moment, as an example vacuuming, releases my flow mind to become focussed on the two things simultaneously, one requires little energy, the vacuuming and the other might be the hyper-focus required to flow through thoughts on leadership or writing this book, or the next coaching session.

Marcus Trescothick, the former England cricketer and captain of Somerset County Cricket Club, described it this way,

> To relate it to my cricketing terms, when you're batting, facing somebody who's bowling at extreme pace, or you're at the highest-pressure moment playing for your country, you're very aware of everything that's going on around you. The feeling of the crowd, the feeling of the pitch, hearing the noises, everything that's happening, but it's almost, (like you know) it's happening, you're hearing it, you're feeling it, but it's going on around you. And you're still locked into what's happening, and that's facing the ball looking, watching the cricket ball.

It is also interesting to consider how long a 'moment' might be. In general terms, it is considered to be a very brief period of time, but sometimes the word holds in it much more, that moment in history when the world changed, for example, 'that's one small step for a man one giant leap for mankind', it was a 'moment', a culmination of years of work, but it was the moment that Neil Armstrong became the first human being to stand on the moon. So, it's within your gift to choose how long a moment is and how you will be *with* it.

Back to Vincent Walsh, he said this when I interviewed him and we talked about Jonny Wilkinson, former England rugby player and probably one of the best fly-halves to play the game,

I'll give you an example of why I think he would get into a flow state and most people never will. I do think it's an issue of courage, and we lose it as we get older, in the same way as we drum the creativity out of children as they get older.

He continued,

Flow is something that is out there, it's in there and you've got to dig deep to get it and, you've got to dig deep for a long time, and it might not be there when you want it to be there, wanting it to be there might be a precondition for it not being there.

He went on to say,

I would see it (flow) as a subjective state that we agree exists. And it's really fantastic when it happens, there might be some good consequence of it. Yet, if one of your teammates had it in the game today then that's great, we can talk about it, but can you use it? Can you learn from it? Is it something that you can pursue?

I think Walsh gives us something that sits alongside curiosity and gratitude, and that is courage and creativity, and there are of course many ways to think about both of those things. Walsh himself is an avid musician. He also thinks, as I do, that it is a deeply subjective thing, and as we have noted, you have to work at it, develop your practice, and heighten your awareness of what might be possible through flow. It's interesting to note his comment earlier, 'let the flow be an emergent property', which begs the question, where does it emerge from?

Marcus Trescothick offers another word that we might add to our flow vocabulary,

I would relate it to a different type of word, which would be contentment. You know, just being at ease with everything that's going on. Flow to me would be something fluid, like water or something, that would relate to me. And I suppose in a way, that if you think about it, that's what you feel when you're at total ease with what you're doing. Everything is moving, like it should do, but also slower than it than it needs to, because it feels like your brain is working at that ultimate capacity at that very moment in time.

So, it is another subjective experience and construing of flow, but one that still talks of its potential to lift us if we tune in to it.

It could be argued that flow extends the self beyond the realms of the known being, into that place of undiscovered potential. We get to meet the best version of ourselves through the complex, dynamic, psychological processes if we have the courage and discipline to pursue something that can't be specifically measured or objectively named, but if it increases our performance in whatever sphere, we are touching our own greatness, the gift of being who we are at our best. And if we can approach the flow opportunity with curiosity, creativity, and contentment, perhaps we are giving ourselves permission to go further than we thought possible, reach heights that we never imagined we could, create a life where we survive and thrive, if not on our own terms, then at least consciously knowing that we can be capable of more with devotion to our direction of travel. As the late educator, Sir Ken Robinson said about self-discovery, 'you can't do this if you are trapped in a compulsion to conform. You can't be yourself in a swarm'.

And perhaps that brings us full circle, back to the source, to be in touch with the fertile, febrile, unfettered being that dwells within us. Complete in the knowledge that if the label doesn't enable, we will not capitulate to it; we will not collude with those people or technologies that would steal our attention from our vision or mission; we will not be complicit or complacent in using our gifts or our flow; and no amount of coercion will tear away at our spirit and reduce us to less than we can be – born to flow.

Summary

In this chapter, we see, consider, and contemplate returning to the source:

- Be mindful of what you are doing in *and* with the moment; there is a difference.
- The way of flow *is* to flow, that is, feel the flow, get lost in your own inner being.
- 'What got you here won't get you there', said Marshall Goldsmith.
- To be the flow, you have to become the flow, to paraphrase Bruce Lee.
- Exercise your flow muscles as you would any other.
- Flow can be a bypass of the conscious mind, an intuitive experience of our way of being, rather than an always deliberate move towards or away from a task.
- Intuition sits lightly on the shoulder of intellect.
- When intuition is allowed room in our mind, we generally tend to *think* differently.
- Intuitive thought or insight is akin to a flow experience.
- Intuition is a trait that we all have. We know we have been intuitive before, we know we are being intuitive in a moment, and we know we will be intuitive again. It's the same with flow.
- Flow is retrievable from the deep recesses of being.

- There is an anticipatory predictiveness when our flow is at its zenith, when thinking is too slow to be optimal, and effortless effort releases us from the thinking mind so that we flow beyond our bounded rationality.
- Flow requires diligence and devotion, till we find that the *trying* has ceased, and the flow way is a constant companion.
- Curiosity and gratitude, for example, are enablers to be happy *with* the moment.
- According to Yamamoto Tsunetomo, 'There is surely nothing other than the single purpose of the present moment. A man's whole life is a succession of moment after moment. There will be nothing else to do, and nothing else to pursue. Live being true to the single purpose of the moment'. Less to do with flow and more to do with appreciation of the now.
- Martha Graham wrote, 'There is a vitality, a life force, an energy, a quickening that is translated through you into action'. Perhaps you could construe her construing as flow.
- We must, paradoxically, see ourselves as the lighthouse *and* be the ship at sea.
- Alongside curiosity and gratitude, cultivate a mind that is mindful of itself and still be with the moment.
- How long is a 'moment'?
- If flow is an emergent property, where does it emerge from?
- It could be argued that flow extends the self beyond the realms of the known being, into that place of undiscovered potential.
- In figure 24.1 we can see What the path of flow might actually be like, in life, devoid of linearity.

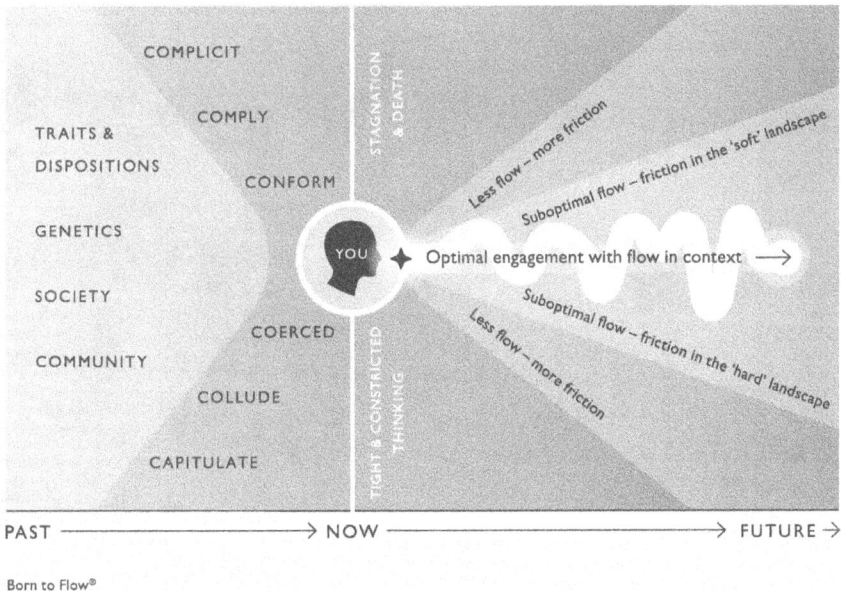

Born to Flow®

Figure 24.1 What the path of flow might actually be like

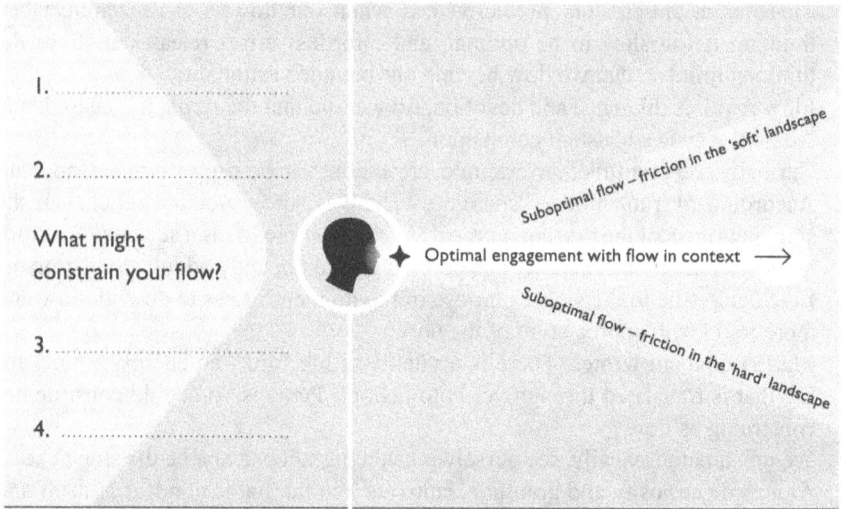

1. ....

2. ....

What might constrain your flow?

3. ....

4. ....

Suboptimal flow – friction in the 'soft' landscape

Optimal engagement with flow in context ⟶

Suboptimal flow – friction in the 'hard' landscape

Born to Flow®

Figure 24.2

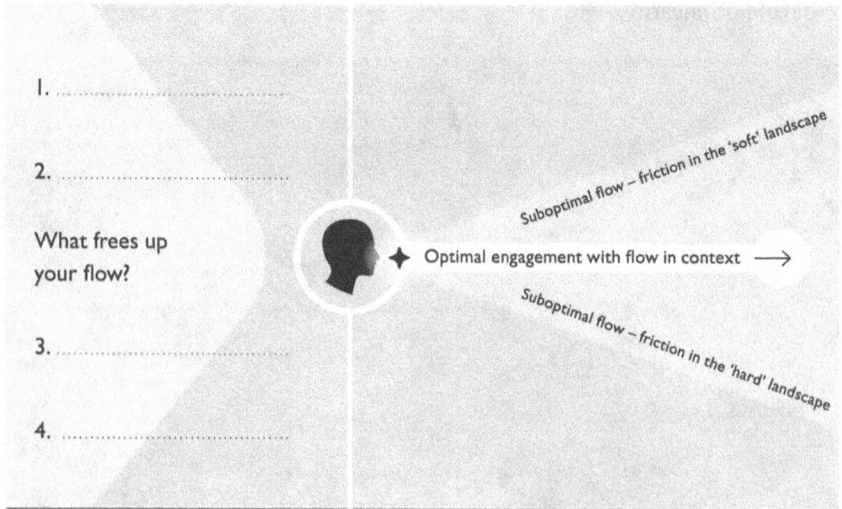

1. ....

2. ....

What frees up your flow?

3. ....

4. ....

Suboptimal flow – friction in the 'soft' landscape

Optimal engagement with flow in context ⟶

Suboptimal flow – friction in the 'hard' landscape

Born to Flow®

Figure 24.3

Exercise/Reflective Practice

'How to harness your flow potential by being in spaces and places that encourage flow to emerge without necessarily connecting it to a specific task' came from the I AM podcast with Jonny Wilkinson when he asked for some ideas on how to enable flow in everyday life:

1 Dispense with the trivial in your life. If it doesn't fulfil you/add value, don't do it.
2 Declutter the agenda that you think you have and create space to flow i.e., reduce friction.
3 Cultivate a mindset that is aligned with the way you want to be in the world. Mindset is a skill; it can be developed and improved.
4 Literally get as close to natural flow as you can, for example, rivers, streams, oceans, or spaces where you can be in touch with nature flowing.
5 Develop a campaign around peak rest and recovery, peak nutrition, peak development/training.
6 Have connections and alignment with a great support network.
7 Align, integrate, and connect with your values as you live and be them (for example, I believe that honour, compassion, empathy, integrity, curiosity, and humility support my flow. I try to live them; I am not always successful but I'm not a saint either).
8 Keep a beginner's mind ('In the beginner's mind there are many possibilities, but in the expert's, there are few', said Shunryu Suzuki (1905–1971)).
9 Cultivate a deep appreciation of the nature, remembering you are part of it, not separate from it. This is connective.
10 Curate an attitude of curiosity in the way you are in the world, add value (if it doesn't add value, why are you doing it?), don't settle, pay it forward.
11 Remember, you contain multitudes. Do not be constrained by contradictory thinking, you have absorbed and experienced much that enables your flow.

Through time, and by definition through life, we rub up against frictions that may slow us (Figure 24.1).

Use the diagram below (Figure 24.2) to understand how you feel and think about things, actions, thoughts that might constrain your flow.

Use the below diagram (Figure 24.3) to help you identify what really frees up your flow and then put an action plan around your outcomes if you haven't already.

Reference

Simon, H. A. (1992). What is an explanation of behavior? *Psychological Science*, 3(3), 150–161.

Words for Flowing

Allowing, Appreciation, Attending, Awareness, Being, Becoming, Campaign, Childlikeness, Clarity, Commune, Confidence, Confluence, Consistency, Construe, Contentment, Courage, Curiosity, Current, Creativity, Devotion, Discipline, Emergent, Enable, Engaging, Evolution/Evolving, Experiences, Expression, Feeling, FLOW, Generative, Gratitude, Growing, Identity, Inspiration, Intensity, Intuitive, Leadership, Legacy, Letting Go, Meaningful, Mind, Mindset, Mind-shift, Motivation, Mystery, Now, Nutrition, Practice, Potential, Performance, Process, Recognising, Recovery, Remembering, Rest, Significant, Simplicity, Subjective, Source, Tao, Tariki, Thinking, Transcendent, Tributary, Unfolding, Zen.

Acknowledgements and Thanks

It would be churlish to have written a book about flow without acknowledging the tremendous contribution Professor Mihaly Csikszentmihalyi made to the field of positive psychology in general, but flow psychology specifically. Whilst I think differently about flow from the way the professor defined it, without his seminal work, *Flow - The Psychology of Happiness*, I would not have gone on my own flow journey, and I would not have written this book. My sadness is that I didn't have the opportunity to engage with the professor before he died in 2021. I am deeply grateful for his work and wisdom.

There are so many other people who have encouraged, cajoled, challenged, and been fantastically generous with their time that I am sure to miss someone out, forgive me if I do. The book is better for their generosity and, of course, any errors are my own.

Firstly, I want to express my deep gratitude to all those that agreed to be interviewed for *Born to Flow*, and whilst not all those interviews made the final draft, their thoughts, time, and contribution were invaluable in helping me shape my thinking.

Laird Hamilton, whose life is literally one of flow is the personification of a 'waterman' and was candid and beautifully generous in sharing his love of the ocean, life, and his experience of flowing. Aloha! Laird. David Hemery MBE, showed his generosity in sharing his thoughts both as an Olympian, and more importantly, as a teacher and coach. Vincent Walsh, emeritus professor, Institute of Cognitive Neuroscience at UCL, was also generous and candid and made a marked impact on the way I considered flow. He had been interviewed in the early stages of writing and researching.

Two elite coaches from the world of rugby added layers that I think only people who understand a full contact sport could – Conor O'shea, director of performance England Rugby, and someone who I am truly honoured to have met and kept a dialogue with over the last few years; Steve Borthwick, gentleman first, elite coach second, and who was kind enough to write the foreword from the unique perspective of elite sport. I also had the good fortune to spend a little time chatting with Jonny Wilkinson, and as a guest on his podcast, 'I AM'. Whilst Jonny will always be remembered amongst England rugby fans for his last second winning drop goal in the 2003 Rugby World Cup, his exploration into all things connected with human potential and performance on his podcast, along with his work at his charitable foundation, shows a commitment to the human endeavour and meeting our better selves that transcends his involvement in sport.

Staying with sport, Marcus Trescothick, former England cricketer and coach, made time to talk about all things related to performance, pressure, and flow. We sat in Somerset County cricket ground stands on a beautiful day, and I was privileged to see a side of an elite athlete that not many people do; again, his generosity in sharing his experience was eye opening. Ann Daniels, polar explorer and world record holder and the first women in history to reach the North and South Poles as part of all women teams, was kind enough to be interviewed with my daughter, Maddie, who was about to embark on her studies in sports psychology accompanying me. Ann understands more than most the link between flow and extreme conditions.

In the realm of sports psychology, whilst not an interview as such, Dave Collins, who was gracious enough to give me his time, answered my questions and pointed out, with candour and care, where I might direct my attention.

Charles Hazlewood is a conductor, composer, and founder of Para-orchestra, the world's first integrated ensemble of disabled and non-disabled musicians, spoke to the nature of his flow with such a melodic elegance that I think will resonate with many. Charles simply vibrates with passion, and we are only touched by vibration.

Justin Hughes, a former Red Arrow and now CEO of Net ZeroNitrogen, was deeply insightful with regard to seeing anomalies in patterns. He began our conversation somewhat sceptical; however, our two hours together caused him to reflect that, 'maybe he was in flow throughout'. Professor Tom Treasure, cardiac thoracic surgeon was generous many years ago when I was writing a screenplay and simultaneously showed me the deep mystery of life and demystified the body, and it was breath taking. As I came to write *Born to Flow*, 'the Prof' was once again generous enough to spend time with me, and I will be forever grateful.

There are many others who contributed to *Born to Flow* in their own way, including Claire Davey, executive coach and former head of coaching at Deloitte, who was kind enough to read an early draft, as did the inimitable David Ross, author of *Confronting the Storm*, and former US Navy Seal, Adam Karoguz, a true Son of Poseidon.

Rufus Harrington taught me grief comes in many forms. Hanshi Kenshu Hideo Watanabe taught me to always drink upstream. Michael 'Yame' Stokes showed me a long time ago how to move the decimal point and Steve Pound does his best to keep it there, Rob Mataic, brother in a different life, Manish Shah, a beautiful human, John Haughey, first and foremost a friend and former Vice-Chair and Global Life Sciences and Health Care Consulting Leader at Deloitte, and one of the best leaders I've had the privilege to work with. John kindly agreed to write a foreword from his global leadership perspective. The late Peggy Dalton, Mike Scott of the Waterboys (although we never made the interview happen, his music has lived with me for a long time, and I have a kind of hiraeth for that lost opportunity),

Andy Fillery, who literally saved my life, and the Kent & Sussex air ambulance service. And inter alia, George Noakes, Professor Mike Tipton, Professor Mark Wilson, Oscar Correia, Rob Cullen, Roy & Mary Harper, Steve Harrison, Kylie Roberts, Mike Berry, Fiona Strongman, Jan Lewis, Henry Odil Nwume, Tim Perrin, the late, great, Robert Posner, Gary Lloyd, Peter Lawrence, Christopher Allen, and Nic Rixon. Mark Walsh & Dellus West, my osteopaths of many years who have helped keep me sane, Sir John Whitmore, Bede Brosnahan, Andrew Cotton, Michael Moore, James Allen, and Rebecca Gwyn.

Aword for Myles Downey, the coaches coach. Myles was to accompany me on this journey; however, circumstances changed, and I journeyed alone, notwithstanding the aforementioned people. Myles, along with John Whitmore, founder of Performance Consultants, probably contributed more to the development of executive coaching with their seminal works, *Effective Coaching: Lessons from the Coaches Coach* and *Coaching for Performance*, respectively, than anyone else in the coaching scene at the beginning. Myles founded the renowned, School of Coaching, in the UK and developed a reputation for a first-class education in executive coaching. Our paths continue to cross, and we speak often of flow, and turning potential into performance.

Big thanks to Anthony 'Tone' Bullen of Smorgasbord Creative – smorg.com.au, for creating the diagrams throughout the book.

Finally, deep gratitude to Iain Faulkner who was generous enough to let me use his painting, *Flow*, for the front cover. This image has accompanied me on the journey of writing *Born to Flow* and captivated me from the first time I saw it. In it I see the protagonist through the mind of Shunryu Suzuki, 'Waves are the practice of the water. To speak of waves apart from water or water apart from waves is a delusion'. Standing on the shore, in harmony, flowfull reflection, nothing exists in isolation.

Flow well, all.

Index

Note: Page references in *italics* denote figures.

For Product Safety Concerns and Information please contact our EU
representative GPSR@taylorandfrancis.com
Taylor & Francis Verlag GmbH, Kaufingerstraße 24, 80331 München, Germany

www.ingramcontent.com/pod-product-compliance
Lightning Source LLC
Chambersburg PA
CBHW070343270326
41926CB00017B/3967